THE ANNOTA~

Groundwork for the Metaphysics of Morals

IMMANUEL KANT

Edited by
STEVEN M. CAHN

Translated by
ANDREA TSCHEMPLIK

Introduction and Commentary by
KRISTA K. THOMASON

Manuscript Edited by
MARY ANN McHUGH

ROWMAN & LITTLEFIELD
Lanham • Boulder • New York • London

Editor: Natalie Mandziuk
Assistant Editor: Deni Remsberg
Higher Education Channel Manager: Jonathan Raeder

Credits and acknowledgments for material borrowed from other sources, and reproduced with permission, appear on the appropriate pages within the text.

Published by Rowman & Littlefield
An imprint of The Rowman & Littlefield Publishing Group, Inc.
4501 Forbes Boulevard, Suite 200, Lanham, Maryland 20706
www.rowman.com

6 Tinworth Street, London SE11 5AL, United Kingdom

British Library Cataloguing in Publication Information available

Library of Congress Cataloging-in-Publication Data

Names: Kant, Immanuel, 1724–1804, author. | Cahn, Steven M., editor. | Tschemplik, Andrea, 1961– translator. | Thomason, Krista K., writer of commentary.
Title: The annotated Kant : Groundwork for the metaphysics of morals / Immanuel Kant ; edited by Steven M. Cahn ; translated by Andrea Tschemplik ; introduction and commentary by Krista K. Thomason ; manuscript edited by Mary Ann McHugh.
Other titles: Grundlegung zur Metaphysik der Sitten. English
Description: Lanham : Rowman & Littlefield Publishing Group, 2020. | Includes index. | Summary: "This new, complete translation of Kant's 'Groundwork' makes a challenging foundational work of moral philosophy accessible to all readers. Remaining faithful to the original German, the text is rendered clearly to promote reader comprehension. An inviting introduction, running commentary, and glossary further support study and interpretation"— Provided by publisher.
Identifiers: LCCN 2019052773 (print) | LCCN 2019052774 (ebook) | ISBN 9781538125939 (cloth) | ISBN 9781538125946 (paperback) | ISBN 9781538125953 (epub)
Subjects: LCSH: Kant, Immanuel, 1724–1804. Grundlegung zur Metaphysik der Sitten. | Ethics.
Classification: LCC B2766.E5 T73 2020 (print) | LCC B2766.E5 (ebook) | DDC 170—dc23
LC record available at https://lccn.loc.gov/2019052773
LC ebook record available at https://lccn.loc.gov/2019052774

CONTENTS

Preface

Steven M. Cahn

Immanuel Kant's *Groundwork for the Metaphysics of Morals* is widely regarded as a philosophical classic. Indeed, anyone taking an introductory course in ethics can expect to be asked to study at least part of it.

Yet the work is formidable. Its vocabulary is unfamiliar, its principles abstruse, and its overall position difficult to summarize. For these reasons, teachers soon realize that a presentation of Kant will test their pedagogic abilities.

While many translations and editions of the work are available, most are more suitable for scholars than beginners. Even with a handful of footnotes or accompanying critical essays, these volumes do little to moderate the difficulties faced by those struggling to understand Kant's thought.

This book is intended to help meet the challenge. First, an accessible introduction provides needed context. Second, the translation itself, while as accurate as possible, seeks to clarify, not complicate. Third and most distinctive, a running commentary and glossary assist the reader in staying on track. As an aid, the annotations are placed on pages opposite the text, with space provided for note taking.

My thanks to Natalie Mandziuk, acquisitions editor at Rowman & Littlefield, who appreciated the importance of this project and throughout its development provided support and guidance. I am grateful to

Andrea Tschemplik for her elegant translation and to Krista K. Thomason for her insightful introduction, commentary, and glossary. Our work was aided at every stage by the editorial insights of Mary Ann McHugh. We are also grateful to senior production editor Patricia Stevenson for her conscientiousness.

We have benefited from the insights of those reviewers, chosen by the publisher, who provided input on this project. They include Melissa Barry, Anne Margaret Bailey, Michael Beaty, Marina Bykova, Louis Colombo, Terry Godlove, Samir Haddad, Andrew Kelley, Christopher Kutz, Dustin Peone, Robert Roecklein, William Schweiker, Patrick Shade, Stephen Sims, Mary Whall, Eric Wilson, and Benjamin Yost. We were significantly aided by the substantial reviews provided by Abigail Doukhan, Daniel Garro, and Gordon Simmons, as well as by the detailed commentaries offered by Cecil Eubanks and Daniel Lindquist.

Our hope is that this presentation of Kant's masterpiece will enable all readers to appreciate the powerful vision this work offers.

INTRODUCTION

Krista K. Thomason

IMMANUEL KANT (1724–1804) IS ONE OF THE CANONICAL FIGURES IN the history of philosophy, and *Groundwork for the Metaphysics of Morals* is one of his best-known works. It is required reading in many philosophy courses, especially those that cover moral philosophy. And for good reason. The *Groundwork* introduces some of Kant's most famous contributions to moral philosophy. Here, Kant articulates his arguments about moral duty and human dignity, ideas that have become influential both in the history of philosophy and more widely in our everyday thinking.

Kant's book, however, does not make for easy reading. He uses technical language and, moreover, appears to presume that readers of the *Groundwork* are familiar with his other treatises, thus giving the impression that they have walked into his arguments in the middle rather than at the beginning.

Our hope is that this edition eases some of the struggle. It is aimed at those who have not encountered Kant previously and may have little acquaintance with philosophy. In other translations, notes provide background context or define an unfamiliar term. Ours also do so, but they do more. They guide the reader through the text, providing a companion to help make plainer some of his dense language, remind the reader where Kant is in his arguments, and offer examples that make concrete some of his more abstract ideas. In this way, we seek to remove barriers while encouraging readers to do their own interpretative work.

Before approaching the text itself, let us consider its context: The *Groundwork* was published in 1785. It appeared four years after Kant's masterpiece *Critique of Pure Reason* (or *first Critique*) and twelve years before the *Metaphysics of Morals*, the book whose groundwork it is supposed to establish. Because the *Groundwork* references the *first Critique*, a few words about that book are helpful.

In it Kant provides a close examination (a "critique") of the discipline of metaphysics, the study of the nature of reality. According to Kant, that study was in crisis, having been attacked as useless, misguided, or even harmful. Kant wants to defend the discipline while convincing the traditional metaphysicians that they have approached matters in the wrong way. Central to Kant's project is determining the limits of reason. Traditional metaphysicians believed that using only their reasoning powers, they could reach conclusions about the most far-reaching subjects, including the existence of the soul, the structure of the universe, or the nature of God. Kant argues that reason cannot prove anything one way or the other about such matters, but it can nevertheless play an important role in expanding our knowledge of the world.

According to Kant, one reason traditional metaphysicians believed they needed to resolve the most fundamental matters is because they believed morality to be at stake. They believed that morality had to be based on the existence of God or the immortality of the soul. Kant, however, denies this connection and seeks to explain the relationship between traditional metaphysics and morality. This question is the starting point for the *Groundwork*, where Kant takes his readers through a progression of reflections about morality. Beginning with what ordinary people believe, he proceeds to offer a philosophical account of what morality is and what it requires of us.

Even though he resists the idea that we need to work out all our metaphysical questions in order to answer moral questions, he is sympathetic to the methods of traditional metaphysics. In the *Groundwork*, Kant often speaks of the need to do "pure" philosophy that is devoid of "empirical" elements, which are derived from experience.

To see why, let us consider one of Kant's own examples: What does it mean to be a good friend? We can go about answering this question in different ways. One approach would be to consider all the available examples of friendship. According to Kant, this method would be empirical. Yet it has flaws. First, we have no reason to think that our examples of friendship are good, not bad. Second, we need criteria to know that a friendship is good. How do we determine the criteria? We cannot do so by surveying all our examples of friendship. That method would be akin to deciding the definition of a good film by watching innumerable films.

Imagine instead that we surveyed what people think. Yet people are sometimes mistaken about the nature of a good friendship. Thus we would learn from a survey only what people generally believe about friendship, not what constitutes the actual nature of a good friendship. Suppose we asked only wise people. This method looks like an improvement because we would be less likely to receive bad answers. Yet how do we decide who is a wise person? We would need to know what makes a person wise. Thus, for Kant, the empirical method seems to lead us in circles.

To determine the essence of a good friendship, we need to think about the definition of a good friendship, which, in Kant's view, is the territory of the metaphysicians. How do we develop a definition? We do what the metaphysicians do: reason about the matter and try to determine the essential characteristics of a good friendship. This is the process Kant uses in the *Groundwork* to examine the nature of morality.

Consider the opening lines from Section 1:

Nothing in the world, or even beyond it, can possibly be conceived and be called good without qualification other than a **good will**. Understanding, wit, judgment, and other *talents* of the mind are undoubtedly good and desirable in many respects, as are the qualities of *temperament* such as courage, determination, and perseverance. But both (the talents of the mind and the qualities of temperament) may also become extremely bad and harmful if the will that utilizes these gifts of nature, and whose constitution is thus called *character*, is not itself good.

How does Kant arrive at this claim about the good will? In spite of unfamiliar language, Kant's reasoning is rather straightforward. Imagine that someone asks you what makes a person good. You might initially think of a list of good qualities or traits. Perhaps you believe that courage makes someone good. Then you consider, for example, a courageous supervillain from a comic book, who clearly is not a good person. The goodness of some qualities or traits seems to depend on the goodness of the person to whom they belong. Being a good person, then, must be something other than just having the right kinds of traits. Whatever "good" means, it has to be (in Kant's terms) good without qualification; it cannot be the sort of thing that can be used in bad ways.

Here we are using the same method that the metaphysicians use. We start with some possible claims. We then try to critique them by identifying their flaws. We switch back and forth between the role of defender and the role of attacker. We do so until we develop claims strong enough to withstand most criticisms. This kind of reasoning does not require us to introduce any empirical element. No data would tell us what is good without qualification. We might begin, as Kant does, with examples of good people and good things familiar to us. But we only use those examples to help craft our definition. To develop it, we leave the examples aside and focus on the definition.

The *Groundwork* proceeds precisely along these lines. In the first section, Kant concludes that whatever "morally good" means, it must be something that is good unconditionally. He suggests that the good will fits this description. All the good qualities and traits we might think of would not be good if they were not in the possession of someone who has a good will. If this claim seems right, then trying to determine what a good will is seems to be the promising next step to figuring out what morality is.

What makes the good will good? According to Kant, central to our understanding of the good will is the concept of duty. Someone with a good will does the right thing *because* it is the right thing to do. Again, Kant thinks a little reflection will prove this point. Imagine two people, both of whom decide to help someone in need. One person explains her actions by saying simply that it was the right thing to do, so she did it. The other person explains that she was hoping her actions would make her famous. Clearly, Kant thinks we judge these two cases differently. The second person has, at best, mixed motives, which makes a difference to us; we do not consider her a moral exemplar even though she ended up doing something good.

We can grasp the idea of acting from duty when we realize that people can do what is right even when they do not want to do so. Think, for example, of a whistleblower who informs the public about the unjust or criminal activity of her employer. She might lose her job; she might be bullied and threatened; she might have her entire life turned upside down. Although she did not want to reveal what she knew, she might reasonably explain that she had to because she felt it was the right thing to do. Against all her desires and interests, she did what was right.

How is this idea possible? From where does this special motivation come? How do we know our duty? According to Kant, our experience with human beings will not answer these questions. In fact, experience would tell us to be pessimistic about this picture of morality. Most people act from mixed motives if they manage to do the right thing at all. Yet, as Kant points out, experience is irrelevant when we think about morality. We are considering what we *ought* to do, not what we in fact do. Notice the uniqueness of such thinking: We are reflecting about what we should do, not what we have done, are doing, or will do.

How are we capable of such reflection? Our closest analog is following a law or a command. Indeed, Kant thinks this approach should seem familiar to us. Return to the example of the whistleblower—she might feel as though she *had to* reveal what she knew, as though her conscience was commanding her. We often experience morality in the form of strong prohibitions. If morality acts like a law, it is not a law like any with which we are familiar. Kant thinks it doesn't come from the state or from God. Instead, it's a law that we give ourselves, coming from our own reason.

In other words, reason grasps the moral law and motivates us to follow it. What does the moral law command us to do? Kant claims that we can't rattle off a list of specific actions, because morality commands us universally. When I think of something that I morally ought not to do, I believe it's not permissible for *anyone* to do. Morality applies to any and all creatures capable of reason, but we all find ourselves in different circumstances. Therefore, the moral law must be general enough to issue commands regardless of the differences in our lives. Such is how Kant arrives at his famous formulation of the moral law (what he calls the "categorical imperative"): Act only on those maxims you can at the same time will should become universal law. When I'm deciding how to act, I ask myself a very familiar question: What if *everyone* did this?

According to Kant, that the moral law applies to everyone also helps us understand what our relationship to each other should be. Morality dictates that when I act, I take into account all my fellow rational creatures. Again, Kant believes this concern will be familiar to us. Most of our moral actions involve respecting other people. We shouldn't lie, cheat, steal, or harm others. We can imagine our fellow humans raising objections: "What if we did that? If you don't think we should be permitted to lie or cheat, then why should you?" We are all, as Kant puts it, "ends" to each other. According to Kant, we see ourselves and all our fellow rational creatures as bound by the same moral law. We are all part of the same moral community (what Kant calls "the kingdom of ends"), in which we all have an equal voice.

This conception of morality is discovered by using the methods of the metaphysicians. Having done so, Kant faces one final question: Is this scheme possible? Perhaps he is right that duty, the categorical imperative, and the kingdom of ends are the right way for us to think about morality. But is it actually so? You can imagine the metaphysicians reading the *Groundwork* and anxiously awaiting the answer to this question. They will likely be disappointed with Kant's answer. Just as he argues in the *first Critique*, if the metaphysicians are looking for a speculative proof, they won't find it. Nevertheless, Kant thinks that metaphysics confirms what common understanding believes.

Return to the example of good friendship: We can develop a definition of a good friend, a standard by which we measure our friendships. If part of being a good friend is being loyal, we will expect our friends to be loyal, and we will be hurt or disappointed if they are not. Even if almost no actual friendships meet our expectations, Kant thinks this condition won't affect the correctness of our definition. The same is true of morality. Acting from duty and respecting others is morally required even if fulfilling those obligations is difficult. Moral life is hard, and people are imperfect. That we don't always do what is right doesn't affect the rightness of what we ought to do. At the same time, we know what is right and that we ought to do it. Yet we also know that many people—even most—fail. Yet neither of these judgments weakens the other.

In other words, we stand between two worlds. In one, we know, thanks to reason, what the moral law requires, and we know that we are capable of following reason because we are free. In the other world, we are tempted by all manner of inclinations to do what we want rather than what is right, and often those inclinations win. Kant believes that we undeniably occupy both worlds. But being a good person requires that we believe the first world can and should influence how we behave in the second.

This conclusion reveals much of what is at the heart of Kant's moral theory. We have to be comfortable living in the tension between the two worlds. No one ever said that being a good person was easy. It requires developing inner strength and good judgment, as we never know what kinds of challenges we will face. We will likely be tempted to act against duty because doing the right thing often requires us to relinquish what we care about or speak up when doing so isn't popular. We are obligated to respect other people even when we may not like them or prefer to do otherwise. In the *Groundwork*, Kant seeks to convince us that we already know what is right and that philosophical reflection confirms our outlook, bringing it into sharper focus. Once we possess that clarity, we can use it to strengthen our resolve and our commitment to acting morally.

Translator's Note

Throughout this translation, I aim to stay as close to the text as possible, eschewing interpretation and using Kantian vocabulary consistent with contemporary scholarship. In an effort to enhance accessibility, I was assisted tremendously by the efforts of Jillian Folger, a sophomore philosophy major at American University, who alerted me to sections that needed clarification. In response, I replaced complex sentences with shorter ones, thereby aiding clarity. I wish to thank her as well as my husband, Jim Stam, for their invaluable help.

This translation is based on Kant's *Grundlegung zur Metaphysik der Sitten* (1785), which is published in volume 4 (387–463) of *Immanuel Kant's Schriften*. Ausgabe der königlichen preussischen Akademie der Wissenschaften (Berlin: W. de Gruyter, 1902).

Andrea Tschemplik

Groundwork for the Metaphysics of Morals

Preface

Ancient Greek philosophy was divided into three sciences: **physics, ethics,** and **logic.** This division, perfectly suitable to the nature of the subject, can only be improved by including its basic principle in order to confirm its completeness and determine its necessary subdivisions.[1]

All rational knowledge is either *material* or *formal.* Material knowledge considers some object; formal knowledge considers the form of the understanding and of reason itself, considers the universal laws of thought in general without distinctions among its particular objects. Material philosophy involves definite objects and the twofold laws to which they are subject: laws of **nature,** whose science is **physics,** or laws of **freedom,** whose science is **ethics.** These are also called *natural philosophy* and *moral philosophy*, respectively.

Formal philosophy is called **logic.**[2] Logic can have no empirical aspect, no part of the universal and necessary laws of thought grounded in experience. Otherwise, it would not be logic, a canon for understanding or reason that is valid for all thought and that must be demonstrable. Natural and moral philosophy, on the other hand, can each have an empirical part, because the former has to determine the laws of nature as derived from experience, and the latter involves the laws of the human will as affected by nature. Natural philosophy features laws according to which everything does happen; moral philosophy addresses laws according to which everything ought to happen. Ethics, however, must also consider the conditions under which what ought to happen frequently does not.

To the extent that it is based on experience, we may call all philosophy *empirical*, whereas *pure* philosophy advances doctrines from *a priori*

1. Some of the material from this part of Kant's preface is borrowed from his previous work and from the work of some of his predecessors. Kant's main point is that ethics has its own domain of inquiry that is different from other subjects.

2. Kant's definition of logic is complex. Generally, he thinks of it as the set of laws that govern human reasoning.

principles alone.³ When pure philosophy is solely formal, it is *logic*; if restricted to definite objects of the understanding, it is *metaphysics*.

Thus arises the idea of a twofold metaphysics: a *metaphysics of nature* and a *metaphysics of morals*. Physics thus has both an empirical and a rational component. So too does ethics, whose empirical part could specifically be called *practical anthropology*⁴ and whose rational part could properly be called morals.

All trades, arts, and crafts have benefitted from the division of labor. Each person who commits to a certain distinctive endeavor is able to perform this work with greater ease and to greater perfection than one person who does it all. Where work is not distinguished and divided, where everyone is a jack-of-all-trades, trades remain primitive. We should consider, then, whether pure philosophy, in all its parts, does not require someone exclusively devoted to it. We should also consider if the whole scholarly trade does not need this, instead of practitioners who, catering to the public taste, routinely blend the rational and empirical elements together without knowing their proportions. While these people might call themselves independent thinkers and call those who engage with only the rational part quibblers, I argue they should be warned not to simultaneously carry on two employments requiring treatments that may differ widely. Each could demand a special talent, whose combination in one person produces only bunglers. I'm simply asking here whether the nature of science should not entail carefully separating the empirical from the rational, and situating a metaphysics of nature before an (empirical) physics proper, and a metaphysics of morals before practical anthropology. Each must be carefully cleansed of everything empirical in order to know how much pure reason can accomplish in both cases [389] and to identify the sources of its a priori teaching, including whether all moralists (who are abundant) expound a metaphysics of morals or only some who feel they have a calling for this enterprise.

4

3. *A priori* is a Latin term that Kant uses to mean "independent of experience." Here and in the subsequent paragraphs Kant is building the case that a metaphysics of morals is possible. Kant will return to this in more detail in Section 2.

4. Kant eventually writes a work on anthropology titled *Anthropology from a Pragmatic Point of View* (1798).

As my concern here is with moral philosophy, I limit the proposed question to this: Is it not of the utmost necessity to work on a pure moral philosophy untainted by anything merely empirical and belonging therefore to anthropology? The possibility of such a philosophy is evident from the common idea of duty and of moral laws. Admittedly, to have moral force as the basis of its obligation, a law must convey absolute necessity. Like other valid moral laws, the command "You shall not lie" applies not just to human beings, as if other rational beings had no need to observe it. Therefore, the source of legal obligation must not be sought in the nature of human beings, or in the circumstances of their world, but a priori simply in the concepts of pure reason. Although any other precept founded on principles of mere experience—even minimally so, perhaps pertaining only to motive—may be in certain respects universal, such a precept can be called a practical rule but never a moral law.[5]

Not only do moral laws with their principles differ essentially from every other kind of practical knowledge featuring anything empirical, but all moral philosophy rests wholly on its pure part. Its application to human beings borrows not at all from knowledge of them (the field of anthropology) but gives laws a priori to them as rational beings. No doubt these laws require a judgment sharpened by experience to determine in what cases they apply and to impress upon the human will their existence, while reinforcing the need to put them into practice. Influenced by so many inclinations, human beings, though capable of the idea of a practical pure reason, cannot easily make this idea concrete and effective in the course of their lives.[6]

[390] A metaphysics of morals is therefore indispensably necessary, not merely for purposes of speculation in an investigation of the sources of the practical principles found a priori in our reason, but also because without this guide and supreme canon for their assessment, morals themselves are vulnerable to all sorts of corruption. For an action to be

5. Kant will defend this point later in the work, but he believes that the nature of morality can never be discovered just by observing what human beings actually do. Morality is about what human beings should do.

6. Kant thinks metaphysics has the right methodology to think about morality precisely because it does not draw on experience. It is "pure" of any empirical considerations.

morally good, it is not enough that it *conform* to the moral law, it must also be done *for the sake of the law*. Otherwise, that conformity is only contingent and uncertain, just as a principle that is not moral, although it may now and then produce lawful actions, will also often produce unlawful actions. Only in a pure philosophy can we find the moral law in its purity and genuineness (and, in a practical matter, this is of the utmost consequence). We must, therefore, begin with pure philosophy (metaphysics), without which there can be no moral philosophy. That which mingles these pure principles with the empirical does not deserve the name of philosophy (for philosophy sets itself apart from common rational knowledge by treating in a separate science what the latter only conceives as mixed together). Much less does it deserve the name of moral philosophy, because this mixture of the pure and the empirical spoils even the purity of morals themselves, defeating its own purpose.

Do not think that what is demanded here is already present in the famous Wolff's propaedeutic[7] to his moral philosophy, namely, what he calls *universal practical philosophy*, and therefore there is no need to break entirely new theoretical ground. Deemed a general practical philosophy, it does not consider a will of any particular kind—such as a pure will, one determined without any empirical motives and solely by a priori [independent of experience] principles—but rather volition in general, with all the actions and conditions its general meaning signifies. His work thus differs from a metaphysics of morals, just as general logic, which treats the acts and canons of thought *in general*, is distinguished from transcendental philosophy, which treats the particular acts and canons of *pure* thought, those whose cognitions are altogether a priori. The metaphysics of morals must examine the idea and the principles of a possible *pure* will rather than acts and conditions of human volition generally, drawn largely from psychology.

7. "Propaedeutic" is used by Kant to mean "introduction." Christian Wolff
(1679–1754) was a German philosopher whose work was influential to Kant
and Kant's contemporaries. The specific text that Kant mentions here is Wolff's
Philosophia practica universalis, methodo mathematica conscripta (*On Universal Practical Philosophy, Composed from the Mathematical Method*), which was
published in 1703.

[391] That moral laws and duty are indeed spoken of in this universal moral philosophy (however inappropriately) does not undermine my assertion, for in this respect, the authors of that science remain true to their idea of it. They do not distinguish the motives that are represented as such by reason alone, altogether a priori, and that are strictly moral, from the empirical motives elevated through understanding to universal concepts merely by comparison of experiences. Without noting their different sources (and viewing them all as homogeneous), they consider only their differing amounts. In this way, these authors frame their concept of *obligation*, which—while being anything but moral—is all that can be attained in a philosophy that passes no judgment whatsoever on the origin of all possible practical concepts, whether a priori or only a posteriori.[8]

Intending to subsequently supply a metaphysics of morals, I issue first this *Groundwork*. Indeed, there is no other proper basis for this metaphysics than the *critical examination* of a *pure practical reason*; just as for metaphysics, there is already provided a critical examination of pure speculative reason. An investigation of pure speculative reason was more necessary than that of pure practical reason, because in moral concerns, human reason can be easily corrected and largely completed, even in the most common mind, while in its theoretical but pure use, human reason is wholly and complexly dialectical.[9] For the critique of a pure practical reason to be complete, it must reveal practical reason's shared identity with speculative reason in a common principle, for these must ultimately be one and the same, distinguished merely in their applications. I could not finish such a critique here, however, without introducing considerations of a wholly different kind, perplexing to the reader. Accordingly, I have adopted the title of *Groundwork for the Metaphysics of Morals* instead of *Critique of Pure Practical Reason*.[10]

A metaphysics of morals, despite its intimidating title, can still be presented in a more popular and accessible form. To that end, it has been

8. *A posteriori* is a Latin phrase used by Kant to mean "dependent on experience," and it is the contrast to *a priori*.

9. The "investigation of pure speculative reason" that Kant mentions here is his earlier work *Critique of Pure Reason*, which was published in 1781, just four years prior to the *Groundwork*. When he talks about a "critique," he means "a critical examination."

10. Kant ended up writing another work under the title of *Critique of Practical Reason* in 1788.

useful to separate this preliminary treatise that lays the groundwork in order not to have to introduce unavoidable subtleties into more straight-forward doctrines.

The present groundwork is nothing more than the investigation and establishment of *the supreme principle of morality*, a study complete in itself that should be independent from every other moral investigation. No doubt my conclusions on this weighty question, not previously examined satisfactorily, would be greatly illuminated by the application of this supreme principle to the whole system of morality and would greatly confirm its adequacy throughout. I must forego this advantage, though, one ultimately more personally gratifying than commonly useful, as a principle's easy applicability and apparent adequacy do not prove its correctness with certainty. Rather, they promote a bias that prevents us from examining and weighing the principle strictly in itself without regard to consequences.

In this work, I have adopted the method I think most suitable, proceeding analytically from common knowledge to the determination of its ultimate principle, and then again going up synthetically from the examination of this principle and its sources to the common knowledge in which we find it employed.[11] The division will, therefore, be as follows:

1. *First section*: Transition from the commonsense knowledge of morality to the philosophical knowledge of morality.

2. *Second section*: Transition from the popular moral philosophy to the metaphysics of morals.

3. *Third section*: Final step from the metaphysics of morals to the critique of pure practical reason.

11. In this sentence, "analytically" means "by investigating the constituent parts" and "synthetically" means "by reassembling the parts." In other words, Kant's plan in the *Groundwork* is to start by taking stock of common moral knowledge, closely examine its foundations, and then return to common moral knowledge with a deeper philosophical understanding of it.

Transition from the Commonsense Knowledge of Morality to the Philosophical Knowledge of Morality[1]

[393]   NOTHING IN THE WORLD, OR EVEN BEYOND IT, CAN POSSIBLY BE CONceived and be called good without qualification other than a **good will**.[2] Understanding, wit, judgment, and other *talents* of the mind are undoubtedly good and desirable in many respects, as are the qualities of *temperament* such as courage, determination, and perseverance. But both (the talents of the mind and the qualities of temperament) may also become extremely bad and harmful if the will that utilizes these gifts of nature, and whose constitution is thus called *character*, is not itself good. It is the same with *gifts of fortune*. Power, wealth, honor, even health, and the general well-being and contentment with one's condition, called *happiness*, yield courage, and often arrogance, if a good will does not correct their influence, rectifying the whole principle of action and adapting it to its universal end. Not to mention that an impartial rational observer can never be satisfied by the sight of a creature who lacks a single feature of a pure and good will but nonetheless experiences constant good fortune. A good will, then, appears to constitute the indispensable condition of even being worthy of happiness.

1. The titles of each of the sections can be helpful. They give some sense of what Kant is trying to do within each section and also how the sections relate to one another. In this section, Kant is surveying what he takes to be common-sense ideas about morality and then subjecting them to philosophical reflection.

2. The opening line to Section 1 is a bit like a thesis statement for Kant; he will defend the claim as the section continues. Kant introduces the concept of a good will here, but he has not yet defined it. In the subsequent paragraphs, he starts to explain it by distinguishing it from other things (e.g., talents, psychological traits).

Certain qualities conducive to this good will may facilitate its work but nonetheless lack intrinsic or unconditional value. Still, they always presuppose a good will, limiting our otherwise proper high esteem for them and preventing us from regarding them as absolutely good. Moderation in emotions and passions, self-control, and calm deliberation are good in many respects and even seem to constitute part of the intrinsic worth of a person, but they should not be called unconditionally good, despite such high praise from the ancients. For without the principles of a good will, these qualities may become extremely bad, and such cold-bloodedness in a villain makes him not only far more dangerous but also more horrible in our eyes.

A good will is good neither because of what it actually performs or achieves nor for its fitness to attain some proposed end, but simply by virtue of its volition, good in itself and esteemed much higher than all that it could bring about in favor of any inclination, indeed even the sum total of all inclinations. Even if it should happen that due to some particular misfortune or the meager provision of a wicked step-motherly nature, this will should wholly lack the power to accomplish its purpose, achieve nothing with its greatest efforts, and leave behind only the good will itself—not as a mere wish, but through summoning all means in our power—then, like a jewel, the good will would still shine by its own light, a thing of complete value in itself neither augmented nor diminished by its usefulness or uselessness. Indeed, its utility would be only a setting to allow for more convenient commercial handling or to attract the attention of aspiring connoisseurs, but not to recommend it to true experts or to determine its true worth.

So inherently strange, though, is this idea of the absolute value of the mere will that takes no measure of its utility, that even if everyone were to support this notion, it might still appear simply high-flown fancy related

[395]   to our misunderstanding of nature's purpose in appointing reason to govern our will. Therefore, we will test this idea from this point of view.[3]

In the natural constitution of an organized being (i.e., one suitably adapted to the purpose of life), we assume, as a fundamental principle, that we will find no organ not the most fit and best adapted for its function. So, if nature's purpose for a being with reason and a will were its *preservation*, its *welfare*—in a word, its *happiness*—entrusting the creature's reason with this goal would have been a very poor decision on nature's part. For all the necessary actions regarding this purpose, indeed the whole rule of the creature's conduct, would be far more surely attained by instinct than by reason. Had this favored creature been granted both reason *and* instinct, the former would have served only to make this being contemplate the happy constitution of its nature, admire it, delight in it, and feel thankful to its beneficent cause. But the creature would not have been given reason to be subject to its weak and delusive guidance and to meddle with nature's purpose. In brief, nature would have ensured that reason should not erupt into *practical use*, nor presume, with its feeble insight, to devise its own plan for and means to happiness. Nature would have taken on the delegation of both these tasks and, with wise foresight, entrusted both solely to instinct.

And, in fact, we find that the more a cultivated reason applies itself purposefully to the enjoyment of life and happiness, the more a person strays from true satisfaction. And hence many people, if candid enough to admit it, feel a certain degree of *misology* (i.e., hatred of reason), especially those most practiced in its use. After calculating all their advantages (derived not from the invention of all the arts of common luxury, but even from the sciences, which also seem after all only another luxury of the understanding), they find that they have, in fact, reaped

[396]   more troubles than happiness. And they ultimately envy, rather than despise, the more common person, whose conduct is guided more by

3. "This point of view" refers to thinking of human beings as creatures who, by nature, are governed by reason. In other words, suppose human beings have been designed by nature to have both reason and a will. What purpose do reason and a will serve?

mere natural instinct and influenced less by reason. Admittedly, those who do not boast of the advantages of reason for producing happiness and satisfaction in life are by no means morose or ungrateful for the goodness with which the world is governed. But hidden at the root of their judgments is the idea that our existence has a different and far nobler end than happiness, for which reason is properly intended and which must, therefore, be regarded as the supreme condition and ranked higher than the private ends of humanity.

Reason cannot competently guide the will regarding its objects and the satisfaction of all our needs (which to some extent it even multiplies), goals better achieved by an instilled instinct. Nevertheless, nature gives us reason as a practical faculty (i.e., one that influences the *will*) and admittedly as a rule distributes capacities adapted as means to an end.[4] Its true purpose must be to produce a *will*, not merely good as a *means* to something else, but *good in itself*, a goal for which reason was absolutely necessary. Such a will, then, though not the sole and complete good, must be the supreme good and the condition of every other, even the desire for happiness. Nature is not inconsistent, although the cultivation of reason, required for the first and unconditional purpose of producing a good will, does in many ways interfere, at least in this life, with the second purpose of attaining happiness, which is always conditional. Happiness may even be reduced to less than nothing, without nature thereby failing its purpose. Reason, recognizing the establishment of a good will as its highest practical vocation, is capable of only its own kind of contentment in the fulfillment of a purpose it determines, even though this may involve abandoning the aims of inclination.

[397]   We must therefore develop the concept of a will highly esteemed as good in itself alone. Already existing in a sound and natural understanding, this concept does not need to be taught but only illuminated. When estimating the value of our actions, a good will always takes first place

4. In the previous paragraphs, Kant believes he has established that our reason is not best suited to helping us attain happiness. Yet Kant thinks reason is practical—that is, it plays some role in our decisions and actions. So, Kant is now faced with the question: What *is* reason's job? Kant answers that it helps to establish a good will.

and constitutes the condition of all the rest. To demonstrate this, we will consider the concept of duty, which includes the concept of a good will, with certain subjective restrictions and hindrances that do not conceal it or render it unrecognizable but rather through contrast make it stand out and shine so much the brighter.[5]

All actions already recognized as contrary to duty, although potentially useful for other purposes, I omit here: The question whether these are done *from duty* cannot even arise, since they actually conflict with it. I also set aside those actions that, while conforming to duty, are performed with *no* direct *inclination* but rather because humans are so impelled indirectly by another motive. For in this case we can readily distinguish whether the action that agrees with duty is done *from duty* or from some selfish objective. It is much harder to make this distinction when the action conforms with duty and the subject also has a *direct* inclination to do it. For example, as a matter of duty, a shopkeeper should not overcharge a naive customer; and wherever business is good, the prudent merchant does not overcharge but keeps a fixed price for everyone, so that even a child can make purchases as well as anybody else. Although customers are thus *honestly* served, we need not believe that the merchant has acted from duty and from principles of honesty, as a self-serving advantage also required it. It is out of the question to suppose that this merchant might also be acting in the customers' best interests and treating them equally out of love. Neither duty nor direct inclination prompted this action, but merely a selfish purpose.

It is a duty, on the other hand, to preserve one's own life; and, moreover, everyone has an immediate inclination to do so. But the often anxious care that the majority of people devote to self-preservation has [398] no intrinsic worth, and its maxims[6] have no moral weight. They preserve their life *in conformity with duty*, no doubt, but not *from duty*. On the other hand, if adversity and hopeless despair have killed all taste for life;

5. This may seem like a quick transition to a different topic, but recall that part of Kant's task in this section is to reflect philosophically on our common-sense moral knowledge. Doing one's duty, Kant seems to think, is a familiar moral experience, and reflecting on it will help him "illuminate" (as he says) the concept of the good will.

6. *Maxim* is one of Kant's technical terms. Roughly, a maxim is a subjective rule of conduct. Precisely how best to understand this term is the subject of some debate among Kant scholars.

if some unhappy person, strong of soul and actively indignant at his fate, rather than passively despondent or dejected, wishes for death and yet preserves his life without loving it—not from inclination or fear, but from duty—then his maxim has moral worth.

To be charitable where possible is a duty, and many people are so sympathetic that, even lacking motives of vanity or self-interest, they find inner pleasure in spreading joy and delight in satisfying others, to the extent that they made this happiness possible. But I maintain that such an action, however dutiful or agreeable, has no true moral worth but remains on a level with actions that arise from other tendencies. The inclination to honor, for example, deserves praise and encouragement if fortunately directed to public utility and in accord with duty and thus honorable, but not esteem. The maxim lacks moral import, that of an action done *from duty*, not from inclination. Assume a humanitarian's own despair clouds his disposition and extinguishes all sympathy with the lot of others. While still capable of helping those in distress, he remains absorbed with his own trouble and untouched by that of others. Now suppose that he tears himself out of this deadly indifference and helps another without any inclination to do so, but simply from duty; only then does his action have genuine moral worth. Furthermore, if nature has endowed the heart of this or that human being with little sympathy; if a person (although upright) is by temperament cold and indifferent to the sufferings of others, perhaps because, enduring his own suffering with the special gifts of patience and fortitude, he presumes—or even demands—similar gifts in others, such a person would certainly not be the worst product of nature. And if nature had not specially shaped this person as philanthropic, would he not still find in himself a source of worth far superior to that of a good-natured temperament? Certainly! For in exactly this way, the moral worth of the character, incomparably the highest of all, is evoked:

[399]   being charitable, not from inclination, but from duty.[7]

7. It might sound from this section as if Kant thinks the morally good person has to be miserable, but that is not his point. Kant is trying to isolate and explain the phenomenon of "acting from duty." He thinks we see it most clearly when we think of people doing the right thing even when they don't want to or don't feel like it.

To secure one's own happiness is a duty (at least indirectly), as discontent with one's own condition, under the pressure of many anxieties and in the midst of unsatisfied wants, might easily become a great *temptation to transgress against duty.* Here again, without consideration for duty, everyone already has the strongest and innermost inclination to happiness, because in precisely this idea all inclinations are united in a sum total.[8] The precept of happiness is often such that it greatly interferes with some tendencies. And yet a person cannot form any definite and certain concept of happiness, the sum of satisfaction of all our inclinations. Not surprisingly, a single inclination, definite in its promise and the time within which it can be gratified, is often able to outweigh such a fluctuating idea. A patient with gout, for instance, can choose to enjoy what he likes and suffer whatever consequences, since, according to his calculation, on this particular occasion, he has not sacrificed the certain enjoyment of the present moment for a possibly mistaken expectation of the supposed happiness of health. But even in such a case, if the general desire for happiness did not determine his will and if health did not figure in his calculations, there still remains in this, as in all other cases, this law,[9] namely, that he should promote his happiness not from inclination but from duty, and thereby his conduct would for the first time acquire actual moral worth.

In this manner, undoubtedly, we should also understand those passages of Scripture that command us to love our neighbor and even our enemy.[10] For love, as an inclination, cannot be commanded, but beneficence out of love itself, even though we are not so inclined and may even be repelled by a natural and unconquerable aversion, is *practical*, not *impassioned* love. Love seated in the will and principles of action, not in the propensities of feelings or tender sympathy, this love alone can be commanded.

8. Kant defines happiness as the satisfaction of all of the totality of our inclinations. Exactly what this means for Kant is a subject of debate among Kant scholars.

9. This is the first place where Kant describes acting from duty as a law. He will return to this idea shortly.

10. This is an allusion to the Bible passages Leviticus 19:18 ("Love your fellow as yourself"), Matthew 5:44 ("Love your enemies and pray for those who persecute you"), and Luke 6:27 ("Love your enemies, do good to those who hate you").

The second proposition[11] is this: An action performed from duty derives its moral worth *not from its purpose* but from the maxim that determines its purpose. Therefore, it does not depend on the fulfillment of the action's objective, but rather on the action's *principle of volition*, without regard to any object of desire. It follows, then, that the purposes of our actions, or their effects regarded as ends and incentives of the will, cannot impart to them any unconditional or moral worth. In what, then, can their worth lie, if not in the will in relation to its expected effect? It cannot lie anywhere *but in the principle of the will* without regard to the ends of such an action. For the will stands at a crossroads between its a priori principle, which is formal, and its a posteriori incentive, which is material. As it must be determined by something, the will must be determined by the formal principle of volition when an action is done from duty, freed of every material principle.[12]

[400]

The third proposition, a consequence of the other two, I would express as follows: *Duty is the necessity of acting from respect for the law.* I may have an *inclination* toward an object that results from my proposed action, but I cannot have *respect* for it, precisely because it is an effect and not an activity of the will.[13] Similarly, I cannot have respect for inclination whether my own or another's. If my own, I can at most approve it; if another's, sometimes even love it (i.e., see it as personally advantageous). Only that connected with my own will as a ground, never as an effect, is worthy of respect, that which does not serve my inclination but outweighs it or is at least excluded from it when making a choice. In other words, only the law itself can be an object of respect and hence a command. Now an action arising from duty must wholly exclude the influence of inclination and with it every object of the will. Nothing remains that can determine the will objectively except the *law*, and subjectively *pure respect* for this practical law, and consequently for

11. Kant does not explicitly identify the first proposition, but it follows from the arguments that he has just made in the preceding paragraphs. The first proposition is that only actions performed from duty have moral worth.

12. The "formal principle of volition" Kant refers to will turn out to be what he will eventually call "the moral law." It is a priori because that principle is something we grasp independently from experience. Since Kant thinks we can act from duty even when we are not inclined to do so, whatever guides the will in these cases cannot be "material" (e.g., a feeling or a desire).

13. We sometimes think of respect as a feeling, but, for Kant, respect is a special sort of moral experience unlike other emotions. He explains this concept in a lengthy footnote.

[401] the maxim* that I should follow this law even to the point of thwarting all my inclinations.

Thus, the moral worth of an action does not lie in its expected result or in any principle of action whose motive is derived from such an anticipated result. For all these effects (agreeable to me or even happy for others) could have other causes and not have required the will of a rational being, where the supreme and unconditional good can only be found. The preeminent good, which we call moral, can therefore consist in nothing other than the *representation of law* in itself, *certainly only possible in a rational being*, in so far as this representation, and not the expected effect, determines the will.[14] This good is already present in the person who acts accordingly, whose first appearance we need not wait for in the result of an action.†

---

*A maxim is the subjective principle of volition; the objective principle is the practical law (i.e., that which would also serve subjectively as a practical principle for all rational beings if reason had full power over the faculty of desire).

†One might well criticize me for taking refuge behind the word *respect* through an obscure feeling instead of replying directly to the question through a concept of reason. Although a feeling, respect is not a feeling *received* through influence but, rather, is *self-produced* through a rational concept and, therefore, distinct from all feelings of the former kind, which may be reduced to either inclination or fear. What I recognize immediately as a law for me, I recognize with respect. This merely signifies the awareness that my will is *subordinate* to a law, without the intervention of other influences on my senses. The direct determination of the will through the law, and the consciousness of this, is called *respect*, thus regarded as an *effect* of the law on the subject, and not its *cause*. The conception of that which infringes on my self-love, respect is considered an object of neither inclination nor fear, although somewhat analogous to both. Only law is the *object* of respect, the law we impose on *ourselves* recognized as necessary in itself. As it is a law, we are subjected to it without asking permission of self-love. As imposed by us on ourselves, it is a result of our will. In the former respect, it is analogous to fear, in the latter, to inclination. All respect for a person is properly only respect for the law (of

14. Kant is making a distinction between two different ways that something can be determined by a law. For example, inanimate objects "follow" laws of causation, but they do not follow these laws because they understand what the law dictates. Rational beings, however, "follow" the moral law in the sense that they understand what it dictates and then determine their wills by it.

[402] But what sort of law whose representation must determine a will, even without considering its likely effect, can be called good absolutely and without qualification? As I have robbed the will of every impulse arising from obedience to any particular law, only the universal conformity of its actions to law in general remains, which alone serves the will as a principle. In other words, I should never act in such way that *I could not also will that my maxim should become a universal law.*[15] Here then the simple conformity to law in general (without grounding it in any particular law applicable to certain actions) serves the will as its principle. Otherwise, duty becomes a vain delusion and a chimerical concept. Human common sense in its practical judgments corresponds perfectly with this, always with a view of the principle suggested here.

Let the question be, for example: May I, when in distress, make a promise I don't intend to keep?[16] I readily concede that this question can signify whether it is prudent or whether it is dutiful to make a false promise. Undoubtedly, the former may often be the case. Indeed, I can easily see that extricating myself from a present difficulty by means of such a promise is not enough. But we also must consider whether this lie may later produce much greater inconvenience than that from which I now free myself. The consequences of my supposed *cunning* cannot be easily foreseen. Trust once lost may damage me more than any ills I currently seek to avoid. We should consider, therefore, whether it would not in fact be more *prudent* to act according to a universal maxim and to make it a habit not to make promises we do not intend to keep. But it immediately occurs to me that such a maxim will nonetheless be based only on the fear of consequences.

---

honesty, etc.) of which we now have an example. Since we also view the improvement of our talents as a duty, we see in a talented person the *example of a law* (namely, to become similarly talented through practice), and this constitutes our respect. All so-called moral *interest* consists simply of *respect* for the law.

15. This is the first appearance of what Kant will eventually call the "categorical imperative." Later in the *Groundwork*, he will refer to it as the "first formula." Commentators call it the "Formula of Universal Law."

16. In the following examples, Kant is attempting to show both (a) that his claims about duty and the will are reflected in how we ordinarily think about them and (b) that his characterization of our moral thinking can tell us why these acts are right or wrong.

Now to be truthful from duty, rather than from fear of harmful consequences, is a wholly different matter. In the first case, the very concept of the action already implies a law for me; in the second case, I must first look elsewhere to see potential consequences for me. Deviating from the principle of duty is beyond all doubt wicked; whereas abandoning my maxim of prudence may often be very advantageous to me, although abiding by it is certainly safer. The shortest and unerring way, however, to determine whether a deceitful promise is consistent with duty is to ask myself: Would I be content should my maxim hold as a universal law? And would I be able to tell myself that everyone may make a false promise in a similar difficulty? Then I soon become aware that while I can lie, I can by no means resolve that lying should be a universal law. Such a law would mean the end of promises, since it would be futile to declare how I intend to behave toward those who would not believe this pretense; or if they hastily did so would pay me back in kind. Hence my maxim, as soon as it became a universal law, would necessarily destroy itself.[17]

[403]

I do not, therefore, need any profound acuity to discern what I must do for my volition to be morally good. Inexperienced in the way of the world, unable to be prepared for all its contingencies, I only ask myself: Can I will that my maxim should be a universal law? If not, the maxim must be rejected, not because of any disadvantage to myself or even to others, but because it cannot become a principle in a possible system of universal law. Reason compels my immediate respect for such legislation. I do not yet have insight about the grounds for this respect (a question the philosopher may investigate). But at least I understand that this is an estimation of the worth that far outweighs all worth of what is recommended by inclination, and that the necessity of acting from *pure* respect for the practical law constitutes duty, to which every other motive must defer, because duty is the condition of a will good *in itself* whose worth surpasses everything.

17. Kant's argument is subtle here. It's not that we can't will lying promises because it isn't wise or prudent to do so. That's a strategic argument, not a moral one. Kant's point is that we can't will the lying promise into universal law because promising would no longer have any meaning at all.

Thus, within the moral knowledge of common human reason, we have arrived at its principle. No doubt, common people do not conceive it in

[404] such an abstract and universal form, yet it is always before their very eyes and used as the standard for their judgments. It would be easy to show how, with this compass in hand, people are able to distinguish in every case what is good and what is bad, what is in accordance with duty and what is not. Without teaching them anything remotely new, we, like Socrates, need only direct their attention to the principle they themselves employ. And for that, to know what we should do to be honest and good, and even wise and virtuous, science and philosophy are not needed. Indeed, we might well have supposed beforehand that the knowledge of what must be done, and what must therefore be known, resides in every human being, within the reach of every human being, even the most common. Here we cannot help but admire the great advantage of practical over theoretical judgment in the common human understanding. In the theoretical domain, if common reason departs from the laws of experience and the perceptions of the senses, it falls into sheer nonsense and self-contradictions, or at least a chaos of uncertainty, obscurity, and instability.[18] But in the practical sphere, it is precisely when the common understanding excludes all sensuous incentives from practical laws that its power of judgment begins to reveal its advantage. Common understanding may then even become subtle, quibbling with its own conscience or with other claims regarding what is right, or wishing, for its own instruction, to determine the authentic worth of actions. In the latter case, common reason may even have as much hope of hitting the mark as any philosopher—almost certainly more, because the philosopher, while not possessing any principle that common reason lacks, may easily be perplexed by a multitude of considerations foreign to the matter that lead it astray. Would it not therefore be more advisable in moral concerns to accept the judgment of common reason and call on philosophy only to render the system of morals more complete and intelli-

18. Kant thinks he has established this conclusion in his previous work *Critique of Pure Reason*.

gible, and its rules more convenient (especially for disputation), rather than deflect common understanding from its happy simplicity or divert it with philosophy onto a new path of inquiry and instruction?

[405] Sadly, innocence, indeed a splendid thing, is not easily maintained and is easily seduced. For this reason, even wisdom—which consists more in conduct than in knowledge—still needs science, not to learn from it, but to secure access to and stability for its precepts. Against all commands of duty, represented by reason as worthy of great respect, human beings feel a powerful counterweight consisting of our needs and inclinations, whose full satisfaction we summarize under the name of happiness. Reason issues its commands unyieldingly, without conceding anything to the inclinations, and with disregard and contempt for these claims, which are so impetuous yet at once so plausible (and which no command can suppress). Hence, there arises a *natural dialectic*[19]—a propensity to challenge these strict laws of duty and question their validity, or at least their purity and strictness, and, if possible, align them more with our wishes and inclinations; in other words, this corrupts their very foundation and destroys their entire dignity, an event that even common practical reason cannot ultimately call good.

Common human reason is thus compelled to go beyond its sphere and step into the field of *practical philosophy*, not to satisfy any speculative need (which it never experiences as long as it is content merely to be healthy reason), but on practical grounds to attain information and clear instruction respecting the source of its own principle and its correct determination in opposition to the maxims based on needs and inclinations. And so it may escape the perplexity of opposing claims and avoid the risk of losing all genuine moral principles through its weakness for equivocation. Even in common practical reason, when it cultivates itself, *dialectic* imperceptibly arises that compels it to seek aid in philosophy. This also occurs in its theoretical use; and in both cases, rest can be found only in a complete critical examination of our reason.

19. *Dialectic* refers to the internal intellectual conflict he describes after the dash. He uses it as a technical term in some of his other works.

Transition from the Popular Moral Philosophy to the Metaphysics of Morals

HAVING DRAWN OUR CONCEPT OF DUTY SO FAR FROM THE COMMON USE of our practical reason does not mean that we have treated it as a concept based on experience. On the contrary, regarding our experience of humans, when they act and refrain from acting, admittedly frequent and justified complaints arise that we cannot identify a single certain example of the disposition to act from pure duty.[1] Although many things are done *in conformity* with what *duty* prescribes, whether they are done strictly *from duty*, so as to have moral worth, is nevertheless doubtful. Hence, there have always been philosophers who denied entirely the existence of this disposition in human actions, ascribing everything to a more or less refined self-love. Yet not questioning, for that reason, the correctness of the conception of morality, they spoke instead with sincere regret of the corruption and frailty of human nature. Though noble enough to take as its rule an idea so worthy of respect, human nature is still too weak to follow this precept. It employs reason, which should serve for making laws, but instead uses it for the interest of the inclinations, whether singly or at most in their greatest possible harmony with one another.

1. Kant has just concluded in Section 1 that duty seems to be the central feature of our everyday experience of morality. In the first few paragraphs of this section, he is raising what he takes to be obvious questions about that conclusion. Surely, he points out, when we observe how people actually behave, we do not see them acting purely from duty; often motivated by ulterior motives, people are weak willed and not especially virtuous.

[407]   In fact, it is absolutely impossible for experience to establish with complete certainty a single case in which the maxim of an action, however right in itself, rested simply on moral grounds and on the conception of duty. Sometimes in even the keenest self-examination, we can find nothing other than the moral principle of duty. This could have been powerful enough to move us to one action or another, and to so great a sacrifice. Yet we cannot surely infer from this that some secret impulse of self-love, under the false appearance of duty, was not the actual determining cause of the will. We like to flatter ourselves by falsely taking credit for a more noble motive, although even the strictest examination cannot completely reveal secret incentives, since questions of moral worth are not concerned with the actions that we do see, but with those inward principles that we do not.

Moreover, we can no better serve the wishes of those who ridicule all morality as a mere fancy of the human imagination that overestimates itself through self-conceit than by conceding that concepts of duty must be drawn only from experience. (From indolence, people are ready to believe this is also the case with all other concepts.) This grants them a clear triumph. Out of love for humanity, I am willing to admit that most of our actions are correct; but upon closer examination, we come upon the dear self, which is always turning up, and it is upon this that the aim of our action is based, and not the strict command of duty (which would often require self-denial). Without being an enemy of virtue, a dispassionate observer, one who does not mistake even the most spirited wish for good for its reality, may sometimes doubt whether true virtue is actually found anywhere in the world. This is especially the case with age as experience makes our judgment wiser and our observation more acute.[2]

This being so, nothing can prevent us from abandoning altogether our ideas of duty and maintaining in the soul a well-grounded respect for its law except the clear conviction that whether actions ever really

2. Kant does not paint an optimistic picture of humanity here. If we were to try to discover the nature of morality just by observing human behavior, Kant thinks we would probably find people misbehaving (or at least acting with mixed motives most of the time).

[408] sprang from such pure sources, or whether this or that takes place, is not at all the question. Reason of itself, independent of all appearances, ordains what ought to take place. Accordingly, actions that perhaps the world has never seen any example of up to now, the very feasibility of which someone who bases everything on experience might greatly doubt, are nevertheless inexorably commanded by reason. Even though a sincere friend might never yet have existed, pure sincerity in friendship is required no less of every person, because, prior to all experience, this duty, as duty in general, lies in the idea of reason determining the will on a priori grounds.[3]

Unless we deny that the concept of morality has any truth or reference to any possible object, we must further admit that its law must be valid, not merely for humans but for all *rational creatures generally*. This is so not merely under certain contingent conditions or with exceptions but with *absolute necessity*. It follows, then, that no experience could enable us to infer even the possibility of such apodictic[4] laws. With what right could we gain unbounded respect as a universal precept for every rational nature if it holds only under the contingent conditions of humanity? Or how could laws of the determination of *our* will be regarded as laws of the determination of the will of rational beings generally if they were simply derived from experience and did not originate wholly a priori from pure but practical reason?[5]

Nothing could be more fatal to morality than trying to derive it from examples. Every example set before me must first itself be judged by the principles of morality to determine whether the example deserves to serve as an original example, i.e., as a pattern; by no means can it authoritatively furnish the concept of morality. Even the Holy One of the Gospels[6] must first be compared with our ideal of moral perfection before we can recognize him as such. He says of himself: Why do you call me (whom you see) good; no one is good (the model of good) except God

3. Recall from Kant's preface that his plan is to provide an account of morality that is a priori, or independent from experience. He has now returned to that argument.

4. *Apodictic* means "demonstrable" or "capable of being definitively proved."

5. In Section 1, Kant argues that reason allows us to grasp morality and to develop a good will. If that is correct, then morality is something we know because we are rational beings and not because we are human beings. Kant conceives of the category of rational beings as larger than the category of human beings: There might be other creatures that are rational, but not human. The result of this argument, according to Kant, is that we cannot derive our understanding of morality simply from observing the actions of human beings.

6. Kant is referring to Jesus Christ.

[409] alone (whom you do not see)?[7] From where do we have the conception of God as the supreme good? Solely from the *idea* of moral perfection that reason draws a priori and connects inseparably with the concept of a free will. Imitation has no place at all in morality, and examples only serve as encouragement, i.e., they confirm the feasibility of what the law commands and make visible what the practical rule expresses more generally, but they can never justify setting aside the true original, which lies in reason. Examples should never be our only guide.

If, then, every genuine supreme principle of morality must rest simply on pure reason, independent of all experience, I think it unnecessary to even ask whether these concepts should be set forth in their generality (*in abstracto*), as they are established a priori along with their corresponding principles, provided they are distinguished from common knowledge and called philosophical. In our times this might indeed be necessary. If we took a vote about whether people preferred pure rational knowledge separated from everything empirical (i.e., a metaphysics of morals) or popular practical philosophy, it is easy to guess which side would win.

This descent to popular concepts is certainly commendable if the ascent to the principles of pure reason has already been accomplished to complete satisfaction. This entails first grounding moral philosophy on metaphysics and then, with this firmly established, giving it a popular *character* to enable access. But it is quite illogical to try to be popular during a first examination, on which the soundness of the principles depends. Not only can this procedure never lay claim to the rare merit of a true *philosophical popularity*, since there is no skill in being intelligible if we renounce all profundity of thought, it also produces a disgusting mish-mash of compiled observations and half-reasoned principles. Shallow minds enjoy this for their everyday chit-chat, but the insightful, feeling confused, dissatisfied, and helpless, look away. Yet philosophers, who easily see through this delusion, are largely ignored when attempting

7. This is a reference to the Bible passages Matthew 19:17 ("Why do you ask me about what is good? There is only one who is good") and Luke 18:19 ("Why do you call me good? No one is good but God alone").

[410]   to turn people from this supposed popularity in order that this acclaim might be legitimate, only after people have gained a definite insight.[8]

We need only look at the attempts to deal with morality favored by popular taste and style, and we shall find in one case the special constitution of human nature (including, however, the idea of a rational nature in general), and in another case perfection, and yet another happiness; here moral sense, there fear of God; a little of this, and a little of that, in a marvelous mixture.[9] It does not occur to ask if the principles of morality are to be sought in the knowledge of human nature at all (which we can establish only from experience); and if not—if these principles are to be found altogether a priori, free from everything empirical, in pure rational concepts only and nowhere else, not even in the smallest degree—to make this method a separate inquiry, as pure practical philosophy, or (if one may use a name so much disparaged) as metaphysics* of morals, to bring this to completeness entirely by itself, and to require that the public, which demands popular treatment, await the outcome of this undertaking.

Such a completely isolated metaphysics of morals—not mixed with any anthropology, theology, physics, hyperphysics,[10] or still less with occult qualities (which we might call hypophysical)—is not only an indispensable ground of all sound theoretical knowledge of duties but also at the same time a desired and needed thing of the highest importance to the actual fulfillment of its precepts. The pure conception of duty and the moral law in general, unmixed with any foreign additions

---

*One can, if one wants, distinguish the pure philosophy of morals (metaphysics) from the applied (namely, to human nature), just as pure mathematics is distinguished from applied, and pure logic from applied. This designation also reminds us that moral principles are not based on peculiarities of human nature but must subsist a priori by themselves. From such principles, practical rules must be derivable for every rational nature and, accordingly, human beings.

8. The aim of Section 1 was to reflect on common moral knowledge. In Section 2, however, Kant argues that we need to go further. To provide a proper explanation for morality, we must turn to philosophical reflection (i.e., metaphysics), as only this method is suitable for examining a priori principles.

9. This list includes some moral theories offered by some of his predecessors. For example, Francis Hutcheson (1694–1746) was a moral sense theorist. One does not need to know the precise details of the theories to understand this part of the text.

10. This term refers to a type of metaphysics that includes supernatural qualities.

[411] of empirical attractions, influences the human heart by way of reason alone (which thus first becomes aware that it can of itself be practical), an influence much more powerful than all other incentives* that may be derived from the field of experience. In the consciousness of its worth, reason despises the latter and can gradually become their master, whereas a mixed ethics, compounded partly of motives drawn from feelings and inclinations, and partly also of conceptions of reason, must make the mind waver between motives that cannot be subsumed by any principle and that lead to good only accidently while also often to evil.[11]

From what has been said, the following is clear: All moral concepts have their seat and origin completely a priori in reason. Moreover, these lie in the most ordinary reason just as much as in the most highly speculative. They cannot be obtained by abstraction from any empirical, and thus merely contingent, knowledge; it is precisely this purity of origin that makes them worthy to serve as our supreme practical principle. To the extent that we add anything empirical, we detract from their genuine influence and from the absolute value of actions. Not only of the greatest necessity from a purely speculative point of view, deriving these concepts

---

*I have a letter from the late excellent Johann Georg Sulzer, in which he asks me why moral instruction, although containing much that convinces reason, still accomplishes so little? My answer, delayed in order to prepare it completely, is simply this: The concepts of the teachers themselves lack clarity, and in their efforts to compensate for this by scaring up motives of moral goodness from everywhere, by trying to strengthen their medicine, they spoil it. The most common observation shows that if we represent an act of honesty performed with a steadfast soul separate from every desire for advantage of any kind in this world or another, and even under the greatest temptations of necessity or enticement, it far surpasses and eclipses every similar action affected, however minutely, by an extraneous incentive. It elevates the soul and inspires our wish for the ability to act similarly. Even moderately young children feel this impression, and one should never represent duties to them in any other light.

11. Trying to construct a metaphysics of morals will (a) clarify our understanding of morality and (b) help us commit ourselves practically to what morality demands. The "mish-mash" of common moral knowledge, according to Kant, sows confusion and can undermine our motivation to do what is right.

and laws from pure reason is also of the greatest practical importance, to present them pure and unmixed, and even to determine the compass of this practical or pure rational knowledge, i.e., to determine the whole faculty of pure practical reason. In so doing, we must not make [412] the principles of morality dependent on the particular nature of human reason, although in speculative philosophy this may be permissible or even necessary at times. Since moral laws ought to apply to every rational being, we must derive them from the general concept of a rational being. In this way, although its *application* to humans requires anthropology, morality must first be treated independently as pure philosophy, i.e., as metaphysics, complete in itself (something easily done in distinct kinds of knowledge). We know well that without such a metaphysics, it would not only be futile to determine the moral element of duty in right actions for purposes of speculative criticism, but impossible to base morals on their genuine principles even for common practical purposes, and especially for purposes of moral instruction in order to produce pure moral dispositions and to engraft these in people's minds for the promotion of the greatest possible good in the world.[12]

In this task we seek not merely to advance by natural steps from the ordinary moral judgment (here worthy of respect) to the philosophical, as has been already done, but also from a popular philosophy (which reaches only as far as it does by groping with the help of examples), to metaphysics, which, unchecked by anything empirical and striving to measure the whole extent of this kind of rational knowledge, goes as far as ideal conceptions (where even examples fail us). We must therefore follow and clearly describe the practical faculty of reason, from the general rules of its determination to the specific concept of duty that springs from it.[13]

Everything in nature works according to laws. Rational beings alone have the faculty of acting *according to* the *representation* of laws, i.e.,

12. In Section 1, Kant argues that we understand duty most clearly by thinking about cases where people do what is right regardless of whether they want to. That assertion anticipates his argument here in Section 2. To truly understand morality, we have to examine it in its "pure" form. That is, we must try to determine what moral principles we could derive from reason alone. Of course, Kant is clear that once we apply those principles to human beings, we have to consider the specifics of human life (e.g., the sort of knowledge anthropology provides).

13. Kant uses the term *practical reason* to distinguish the kind of reasoning we apply in moral cases and when acting. Practical reason differs from theoretical reason, the kind of reasoning that occurs when forming beliefs about the world.

according to principles, or a *will*. Since the derivation of actions from principles requires *reason*, the will is nothing but practical reason. If reason determines the will without exception, then the actions of such a being, which are recognized as objectively necessary, are also subjectively necessary. The will is a faculty to choose only *that* which reason independent of inclination recognizes as practically necessary, i.e., as good. But if reason of itself does not sufficiently determine the will, if the latter is subject also to subjective conditions (particular incentives) that do not always coincide with the objective conditions, in other words, if the will [413] does not *in itself* completely accord with reason (as is actually the case with human beings), then the actions objectively recognized as necessary are subjectively contingent. The determination of such a will, then, according to objective laws is *obligation*, i.e., the relation of the objective laws to a will not thoroughly good is represented as the determination of the will of a rational being by grounds of reason, to which the will is not by nature necessarily obedient.[14]

The representation of an objective principle, in so far as it is obligatory for a will, is called a command (of reason), and the formula of the command is called an **imperative**.

All imperatives are expressed by the word *ought*, indicating the relation of an objective law of reason to a will, whose subjective constitution is not necessarily determined by that law. Laws say that something would be good to do or to refrain from doing, but they say this to a will that does not always do something because it is represented to it as good to do. That which is practically *good*, however, determines the will by means of the representations of reason, and consequently not from subjective causes, but objectively, i.e., on grounds valid for every rational being as such. It is distinguished from the pleasant, that which influences the will only by means of sensation from merely subjective causes, valid only for

14. Many of the finer points in this paragraph are the subject of debate among Kant scholars. Generally, Kant explains that practically rational beings determine their own wills—one of the defining features of rationality. In contrast to non-rational beings who, for example, act primarily on instinct, rational beings must decide for themselves on what basis they will act. If reason determines the will, it does so by giving the will a law or a principle to follow (what Kant refers to as the "objective law").

the sense of this or that person and not as a principle of reason, which holds for everyone.*

[414]   A perfectly good will would therefore be equally subject to objective laws (namely, laws of good) but could not be conceived as forced by them to act lawfully, because the will can be determined to act from its own subjective constitution only by representation of the good. Therefore, no imperatives hold for the *divine* will or in general for a *holy* will.[15] *Ought* is out of place here, because the *volition* is already of itself necessarily in unison with the law. Hence, imperatives are only formulas to express the relation of objective laws of all volition to the subjective imperfection of the will of this or that rational being, for example, the human being.

Now, all *imperatives* command either *hypothetically* or *categorically*. Hypothetical imperatives represent the practical necessity of a possible action as a means to something else that is willed (or at least possibly willed). The categorical imperative would represent an action as necessary of itself without reference to another end, thus objectively necessary.

---

*The dependence of the faculty of desire on sensations is called "inclination" and, accordingly, always indicates a need. The dependence of a contingently determinable will on principles of reason, called an *interest*, is thus found only in the case of a dependent will that does not always of itself conform to reason. In the Divine will, we cannot conceive any interest. But the human will can also *take an interest* in a thing without therefore acting *from interest*. The first signifies the *practical* interest in the action; the second, the *pathological* interest in the object of the action. The former indicates only dependence of the will on principles of reason in themselves; the latter, dependence on principles of reason for the sake of inclination, reason supplying only the practical rule as to how the requirement of the inclination may be satisfied. In the first case, the action interests me; in the second, the object of the action interests me (because I find it pleasant). The first section showed that we must not look to the interest in the object with an action done from duty, but only to the action itself and its rational principle (namely, the law).

15. A rational will is not the same as a perfectly rational will. According to Kant, a perfectly rational will would be like the will of God. Unlike other rational beings, whose motives can conflict with doing the morally right thing, God would not experience the demands of morality as an imperative or a command; He would just act rightly without any internal resistance.

Since every practical law represents a possible action as good and, therefore, necessary for a subject whose actions are determined by reason, all imperatives are formulas determining an action as necessary according to the principle of a will that is good in some respects. If the action is good only as a means *to something else*, then the imperative is *hypothetical*; if represented as *good in itself* and hence necessary, the principle of a will that in itself conforms to reason, then it is *categorical*.

Thus the imperative declares which actions possible through me would be good and presents the practical rule in relation to a will that does not directly perform an action simply because it is good, whether because the subject does not always know that it is good or because, even if it knows this, its maxims might still be opposed to the objective principles of practical reason.

[415]

The hypothetical imperative thus claims only that the action is good for some purpose, *possible* or *actual*. In the first case, it is a **problematical** practical principle, in the second, **assertorical**. The categorical imperative that pronounces an action objectively necessary in itself without reference to any purpose, without any other end, is valid as an **apodictic** (practical) principle.[16]

Whatever is possible only by the power of some rational being may also be represented as a possible purpose of some will. Therefore, the principles of action regarding the means necessary to attain some possible purpose are in fact infinitely numerous. All sciences have a practical part, consisting of problems expressing some possible end and imperatives directing its achievement. These may, therefore, be called in general imperatives of **skill**. Here the question is not whether the end is rational and good, but only what one must do in order to attain it. The precepts for the physician to make his patient thoroughly healthy, and for a poisoner to ensure certain death, are of equal value in this respect, as each serves to realize its purpose perfectly. Because in early youth, it

16. The terms *problematical, assertorical*, and *apodictic* are used in Kant's early works. They are different kinds of logical judgments. Problematical judgments are judgments that might be the case, assertorical judgments are those that are in fact the case, and apodictic judgments are those that must be the case.

cannot be known what is likely to occur to us in the course of life, parents seek to have their children taught a *great many things* and provide for their *skill* in the means for all sorts of *arbitrary* ends. Parents cannot determine which of these their child may aim at, but it is *possible* that the child might aim at them. So great is this concern that they often neglect to form and correct their children's judgment as to the value of things they have chosen as goals.[17]

There is *one* end, however, that we may presuppose for all rational beings (insofar as imperatives apply to them, namely, as dependent beings). Therefore, there is one purpose that they not merely *could* have, but that we may with certainty presuppose they all actually *do have* by a natural necessity, and that purpose is *happiness*.[18] The hypothetical imperative that represents the practical necessity of an action as a means to advance happiness is **assertoric**. It should not be presented as necessary for an uncertain and merely possible purpose, but rather for a purpose

[416]   presupposed with certainty and a priori in every human being, because it belongs to our essence. Skill in the choice of means to our own greatest well-being may be called *prudence*,* in the narrowest sense. Thus the imperative that refers to the choice of means to one's own happiness, i.e., the precept of prudence, is still always *hypothetical*. The action is not commanded absolutely but only as means to another purpose.

Finally, there is one imperative that commands a certain conduct immediately, without the attainment of any other purpose as its condition. This imperative is **categorical**. It does not concern the matter of the

---

*The word *prudence* is taken in two senses, that of both worldly and private prudence. The former involves our ability to influence others so as to use them for our own purposes. The latter is the insight to combine all these purposes for our own lasting advantage. The worth of even the former is properly reduced to the latter, and when people are prudent in the former sense, but not in the latter, we might better say that they are clever and cunning but, on the whole, imprudent.

17. Kant talks about imperatives of skill here but largely leaves them aside for the rest of the work. The primary point is that we must take certain steps to accomplish our goals (Kant uses the term *ends*). Knowing these necessary steps does not tell us whether that goal is good or bad. For example, a knowledgeable chemist could make healing drugs or poison, but her skill set would be the same in both cases.

18. Rational beings can have any number of different ends whose imperatives of skill vary. Happiness is an end all rational beings pursue just by virtue of being the sorts of creatures that we are, but that does not mean that they seek happiness as a moral imperative.

action or its intended result, but rather its form and the principle of which it is itself a result. What is essentially good in it consists in its disposition, whatever the consequences. This may be called the imperative of **morality**.

Volition in accordance with these three kinds of principles is also clearly distinguished by the *difference* of the obligation of the will.[19] To mark this difference more clearly, I think they would be most suitably named in their order if we said they are either *rules* of skill, or *counsels* of prudence, or *commands* (*laws*) of morality. For only *law* involves the concept of an *unconditional* and objective *necessity*, which is consequently universally valid. Commands are laws that must be obeyed, that is, must be followed, even when against inclination. *Giving counsel* involves necessity, but a necessity that can only hold under a contingent subjective condition, namely, whether this or that human being counts this or that as part of his happiness. The categorical imperative, on the contrary, is not limited by any condition, and since it is absolute, although practically necessary, may quite strictly be called a command. We might also call the first kind of imperatives *technical* (belonging to art), the second *pragmatic** (belonging to welfare), the third *moral* (belonging to free conduct generally, i.e., to morals).

[417]

Now arises the question, how are all these imperatives possible? This question does not demand knowing how we can think about performing the action the imperative commands, but merely how we can think about the obligation of the will the imperative expresses in setting the task. No special explanation is needed to show how an imperative

---

*It seems to me that the word *pragmatic* may be most accurately defined this way. For sanctions called such flow properly not from the rights of states as necessary laws, but from provision for the general welfare. A history written pragmatically makes us prudent and instructs the world how to provide for its interests better or at least as well as in former times.

19. In other words, Kant suggests that each imperative determines our wills in different ways. Imperatives of skill provide sets of rules to follow. Hypothetical imperatives function similarly to good advice or wise counsel. Categorical imperatives produce commands.

of skill is possible. Whoever wills the end also wills the means in their power indispensably necessary for it (so far as reason has decisive influence on their actions). Regarding the volition, this proposition is analytic; in willing an object as my effect, we already consider the causality of myself an acting cause. The use of the means is already conceived, and the imperative derives the concept of actions necessary to this end from the concept of the willing of an end. Synthetic propositions must no doubt be employed in defining the means to a proposed end, but they do not concern its ground, the act of the will, but rather its object and its realization.[20] To bisect a line on an unerring principle, I must draw from its extremities two intersecting arcs. Mathematics undoubtedly teaches this only through synthetic propositions. But if I know that the intended operation can be performed only with this process, if I fully will the operation, I also will the action required for it, then that is an analytic proposition; for it is one and the same thing to conceive something as an effect that I can produce in a certain way and to conceive myself as acting in this way.

If it were only as easy to provide a determinate concept of happiness, the imperatives of prudence would correspond exactly with those of skill and would likewise be analytic. For in this case as in that, it could be said: [418] Whoever wills the end also wills (necessarily according to reason) the particular means thereto in their power. But, unfortunately, the concept of happiness is so indeterminate that, although we all wish to attain it, we never can say definitely and harmoniously with ourselves what it is we really wish and will. This is because all elements that belong to the notion of happiness are altogether empirical, i.e., they must be derived from experience; and nevertheless, the idea of happiness requires an absolute whole, a maximum of welfare in my present and all future circumstances. Now it is impossible that the most clearsighted and at the same time most resourceful (yet finite) being should form a definite concept of what

20. The distinction between *analytic* and *synthetic* propositions is something Kant argues for in the *Critique of Pure Reason*. Although Kant scholars debate this distinction, here Kant simply means that it is not a great mystery how imperatives of skill are possible. If you have decided to accomplish a task, you judge that you must take the steps needed to accomplish that task. In this case, what it means to will an end is to will taking the steps necessary to achieve that end.

one really wills here. Does one will wealth? How much anxiety, envy, and harassment might we not thereby bring down upon our shoulders? Does one will knowledge and insight? Perhaps this might prove to be only a sharp eye to show us so much more horribly currently concealed, unavoidable ills and to impose more wants on our desires, which already give us enough concern. Will I have long life? Who guarantees that would not be a long misery? Would I at least have health? How often has infirmity of the body restrained me from excess that perfect health would have allowed? And so on. In short, one is unable, on any principle, to determine with certainty what would make one truly happy, because to do so, one would need to be omniscient. We cannot therefore act on any definite principles to secure happiness but only on empirical counsels of, for example, diet, frugality, courtesy, reserve, etc. that experience teaches on average promote well-being. Hence it follows that the imperatives of prudence do not, strictly speaking, command at all, i.e., they cannot present actions objectively as practically *necessary*; they are to be regarded as advice (*consilia*) rather than commands (*praecepta*) of reason, and the problem of determining surely and universally what action would promote the happiness of a rational being is completely insoluble. Consequently, no imperative respecting happiness is possible that should, in the strict sense, command us to do what makes us happy. Happiness is not an ideal of reason but of the imagination, resting solely on empirical

[419] grounds; and it is futile to expect these to determine an action by which one could attain the totality of a series of consequences that is really endless. This imperative of prudence would, however, be an analytically practical proposition if we assume the means to happiness could be specified with certainty.[21] The imperative of prudence is distinguished from the imperative of skill only by this: In the latter, the end is merely possible, whereas in the former, it is given. Since both only command the means to that which we presuppose to be willed as an end, it follows that

21. Imperatives of skill are analytic because willing a particular end means willing the means to realize it. As Kant points out, achieving happiness is not the same as achieving a particular end. Since we don't know what will make us happy, the best we can do is try to attain happiness given the limited information and experience available to us.

the imperative that commands the willing of the means to those who will the end is in both cases analytic. Thus, there is no difficulty envisioning the possibility of such an imperative.

On the other hand, the question of how the imperative of *morality* is possible is undoubtedly one, the only one, demanding a solution, because it is not at all hypothetical, and the objectively represented necessity cannot rest on any presupposition as with hypothetical imperatives.[22] Here we must always consider that we *cannot* establish *by any example*, i.e., empirically, whether there is such an imperative at all. Instead, we should suspect that all those that seem categorical may yet be fundamentally hypothetical. For instance, if "You should not make a false promise" is stated and assumed to be not mere advice to avoid some other evil—in other words: "You should not make a false promise, lest, if it became known, you would destroy your credit"—then such an action must be regarded as evil in itself, and the imperative of the prohibition, categorical, but we cannot show with certainty in any example that the will was determined solely by the law without any other incentive for action, although it may appear to be so. For it is always possible that fear of disgrace, perhaps also an obscure dread of other dangers, may have a secret influence on the will. Who can prove by experience the nonexistence of a cause when all experience tells us is that we do not perceive it? But in such a case, the so-called moral imperative, which as such appears to be categorical and unconditional, would in reality be only a pragmatic precept, drawing our attention to our own interests and merely teaching us to consider these.[23]

[420] We must therefore investigate a priori the possibility of a *categorical* imperative, for we lack in this case the advantage of experience demonstrating its reality so that its possibility should be necessary only for its explanation, not for its establishment. In the meantime, we can already see that the categorical imperative alone can be stated as a practical **law**.

22. Categorical imperatives present a genuine mystery: How are these possible?

23. We cannot determine how categorical imperatives are possible based on experience alone. Given Kant's earlier claims about people often acting from mixed motives, what might appear at first to be categorical imperatives may be merely hypothetical imperatives in disguise.

All the rest may indeed be called *principles* of the will but not laws, since whatever is only necessary for the attainment of some arbitrary purpose may be considered in itself contingent, and we can at any time be free from the command if we give up the purpose. Conversely, the unconditional command leaves the will no leeway to choose the opposite, and consequently, it alone entails that necessity required of a law.[24]

Secondly, in the case of this categorical imperative or law of morality, the source of difficulty (of having insight into its possibility) is great. This imperative is an a priori synthetic practical proposition;* and given that seeing the possibility of speculative propositions of this kind is so difficult, we can suppose that the difficulty with practical positions will be no less.

With this problem, we will first inquire whether the mere concept of a categorical imperative may not perhaps also supply us with the formula containing the proposition that alone can be a categorical imperative. Even if we know how such an absolute command can be stated, learning how it is possible will require further special and laborious efforts, which we postpone to the last section.[25]

When I think of a *hypothetical* imperative in general, I do not know beforehand what it will contain until I am given its condition. But when I think of a *categorical* imperative, I know at once what it contains. Because the imperative includes, in addition to the law, only the necessity

---

*I connect a priori, and therefore necessarily, the act with the will, without presupposing any condition resulting from any inclination (though only objectively, thus assuming the idea of reason with full power over all subjective motives). This is accordingly a practical proposition, which does not derive the willing of an action by mere analysis from another already presupposed. We have no perfect will, but one that connects the action directly with the concept of the will of a rational being as something not contained in the concept.

24. Categorical imperatives do not present themselves to our wills as optional. They are laws because they command like laws.

25. Kant has now decided to split his question about the possibility of the categorical imperative into two inquiries: establishing a categorical imperative as a coherent concept, and then determining whether it is possible for human beings to act on it.

[421]   that the maxim* shall conform to this law, whereas the law includes no conditions restricting it, only the general statement that the maxim of the action should conform to a universal law remains, and this conformity alone, the imperative properly represents as necessary.[26]

There is, consequently, only one categorical imperative, namely, this: *Act only on that maxim you can at the same time will should become a universal law.*[27]

Now if all imperatives of duty can be deduced from this one imperative as from their principle, then, although the question of whether or not duty is merely an empty concept remains undecided, we shall nonetheless be able to show what we understand by this concept and what it means.

Since the universality of the law according to which effects happen constitutes what is properly called *nature* in the most general sense (as to form), i.e., the existence of things so far as that is determined by general laws, then the imperative of duty may also be expressed thus: *Act as if the maxim of your action were to become by your will a **universal law of nature**.*[28]

We will now enumerate a few duties, adopting the usual division of them into duties to ourselves and to others, as well as perfect and imperfect duties.†

---

*A maxim, a subjective principle of action, must be distinguished from the objective principle—namely, practical law. The former contains the practical rule determined by reason according to the conditions of the subject (often its ignorance or its inclinations). It is the principle on which the subject acts, but the law is the objective principle valid for every rational being, the principle on which we ought to act, i.e., an imperative.

†It must be noted at this point that I reserve the division of duties for a future *metaphysics of morals*. I present it here as arbitrary in order to arrange my examples. For the rest, I understand a perfect duty as one that admits no exception in favor of inclination. I have, then, not merely external but also internal *perfect duties*. This is contrary to the use of the word adopted in schools, but I do not intend to justify this here, as it is all the same for my purposes whether it is acknowledged or not.

26. Recall that in Section 1, Kant introduces maxims (principles of action that individuals form for themselves). Unlike categorical imperatives, maxims are subjective principles of action. Categorical imperatives are objective and hold for all rational beings.

27. Although Kant has been suggesting that there could be multiple categorical imperatives, he now argues that only one exists. The categorical imperative is the law that constrains the subjective principles of action (maxims) that we are permitted to act on.

28. Kant scholars are divided about whether this additional formulation adds something new to Kant's discussion.

1. A person reduced to despair by a series of misfortunes feels sick of

[422]   life but is still in sufficient possession of his reason that he can ask himself whether taking his own life is contrary to his duty to himself. Now he inquires whether the maxim of his action could become a universal law of nature, his maxim being: "From self-love, I adopt a principle of shortening my life when lengthening it will likely bring more ill than pleasantness." The question, then, is simply whether this principle of self-love can become a universal law of nature. We see at once that a law of nature including a law to destroy life, by means of the very feeling whose special nature is to stimulate the furtherance of life, would contradict itself. Therefore, such a maxim could not exist as a universal law of nature and, consequently, would contradict the supreme principle of all duty.[29]

2. Another person finds himself forced by necessity to borrow money. He knows that he will not be able to repay it but also sees that nothing will be lent to him without his firm promise to do so within a fixed time. He wants to make this promise but still has enough conscience to ask: "Is it not unlawful and inconsistent with duty to get out of a difficulty in this way?" Suppose, however, that he resolves to make the promise. Then the maxim of his action would be expressed this way: "When I believe I need money, I will borrow money and promise to repay it, although I know that this will never happen." This principle of self-love or of personal advantage may perhaps be consistent with my entire future welfare, but the question is now, "Is it right?" Changing the claim of self-love into a universal law, I state the question this way: "How would it be if my maxim were a universal law?" Then I see at once that it could never hold as a universal law of nature but would necessarily contradict itself. Supposing a universal law that everyone, when perceiving they are in a difficulty, should be able to promise whatever they please, not intending to keep it, the promise itself would become impossible, as well as the

74

29. Kant's example recalls his comments about the sad philanthropist from Section 1.

end that one might envision in it, since no one would regard anything as actually promised and would ridicule all such statements as vain pretense.

[423]   3. A third person finds in himself a talent that, with some cultivation, might make him a useful person in many respects. But he finds himself in comfortable circumstances and prefers to indulge in pleasure rather than take pains in enlarging and improving his happy natural capacities. He asks, however, whether his maxim of neglecting his natural gifts, in addition to agreeing with his propensity to amusement, also agrees with what is called duty. He sees, then, that a system of nature could indeed subsist with such a universal law although men (like the South Sea islanders) would let their talents rust and resolve to devote their lives merely to idleness, amusement, and procreation, in a word, to enjoyment. But he cannot possibly **will** that this should be a universal law of nature or be instilled in us as such by a natural instinct. For, as a rational being, he necessarily wills that his faculties be developed, since they serve him and have been given to him for all sorts of possible purposes.[30]

4. A fourth person, for whom it is going well, upon seeing that others must struggle with great hardships with which he could help, thinks: "What does it matter to me? Let everyone be as happy as Heaven pleases or as they can make themselves; I will take nothing from them, nor even envy them, only I do not wish to contribute anything to their welfare or help them in distress!" No doubt if such a mode of thinking were a universal law, the human race might very well still survive and doubtless even better than in a state in which everyone babbles about sympathy and good will or even takes care to occasionally put it into practice but also cheats when they can, sells out the rights of human beings, or otherwise violates them. Although it is possible that a universal law of nature might exist in accordance with such a maxim, it is impossible to **will** that such a principle should have the universal validity of a law of nature. For such a will would contradict itself, as many cases might occur in which

76

30. This case is the subject of some debate in Kant scholarship, but, like the other cases, we shouldn't read it as a prudential or strategic argument. Kant seems to argue that there is something about rational nature itself that prevents us from willing that we not develop our talents.

we would need the love and sympathy of others, and by such a law of nature emanating from our own will, we would deprive ourselves of all hope of the aid we then desire.

[424]

These are a few of the many actual duties, or at least what we regard as such, that obviously fall into two classes on the single principle we have presented. We must be *able to will* that a maxim of our action should be a universal law. This is the canon of the moral judgment of the action generally. Some actions are of such a character that their maxim cannot without contradiction be even *conceived* as a universal law of nature, far from it being possible that we should *will* that it *should* be so. In others without this intrinsic impossibility, it is still impossible to *will* that their maxim should be raised to the universality of a law of nature, because such a will would contradict itself. It is easily seen that the former violates strict or rigorous (inflexible) duty; the latter, only more lax (meritorious) duty.[31] Thus it has been fully demonstrated how all duties, in regard to the nature of the obligation (not the object of the action), depend on this single principle.[32]

Observing ourselves in any transgression of duty, we shall find that we in fact do not will that our maxim should be a universal law, for that is impossible for us. On the contrary, we will that the opposite should remain a universal law, even though we assume the liberty of making an *exception* in our own favor or (just for this time only) in favor of our inclination. Consequently, if we considered all cases from one and the same point of view, namely, that of reason, we would find a contradiction in our own will, namely, that a certain principle should objectively be necessary as a universal law and yet would not subjectively be universal but permit exceptions. As, however, we at one moment regard our action from the point of view of a will wholly conformed to reason and then from the perspective of a will affected by inclination, there is not really any contradiction, but rather a resistance (*antagonismus*) of

31. This is a reference to the perfect/imperfect distinction that Kant introduces prior to the example and that he explains in his footnote.

32. Readers sometimes assume that we cannot will the world of lying promises, uncultivated talents, or not helping others when they need it because doing so would yield bad consequences. This is not what Kant means. As he states in this paragraph, the maxims fail because we either cannot (a) conceive of the maxim as a universal law or (b) rationally will that the maxim becomes a universal law. For instance, I cannot rationally will the world of not helping others while at the same time recognizing that, as a rational being, I shall at some point in my life need the help and sympathy of other people. It makes no sense for me to will away something I know I need.

inclination to the command of reason, whereby the universality of the principle is changed into mere general validity (*generalitas*), so that the practical principle of reason meets the maxim halfway. Now, although this cannot be justified in our own impartial judgment, it proves that we actually do recognize the validity of the categorical imperative and (with all respect for it) allow ourselves only a few exceptions we think unimportant and forced upon us.[33]

[425]   We have thus established at least this much: If duty is a concept to have any significance and real legislative authority for our actions, it can be expressed only in categorical and not at all in hypothetical imperatives. Of similar importance, we have shown clearly and definitely the content of the categorical imperative for every practical application, which must contain the principle of all duty, if such a thing exists. We have not yet, however, advanced so far as to prove a priori that there actually is such an imperative, that there is a practical law that commands absolutely of itself and without any other incentives, and that following this law is duty.[34]

In order to attain this proof, it is extremely important to remember that we must not allow ourselves to deduce the reality of this principle from the *particular qualities of human nature*. Duty ought to be a practical, unconditional necessity of action. It must therefore hold for all rational beings (those to whom an imperative can apply), and *for this reason only*, it must also be a law for all human wills. In contrast, whatever is deduced from the particular natural dispositions of humanity, from certain feelings and propensities, or indeed even, if possible, from any special tendency of human reason is not necessarily so for the will of every rational being. This may indeed supply us with a maxim, but not with a law; with a subjective principle on which we may have a propensity and inclination to act, but not with an objective principle on which we should be *directed* to act, even if all our propensities, inclinations, and natural tendencies were opposed

33. Kant thinks that examples of common moral transgressions confirm what he has argued. When we do the wrong thing, it's typically because we make exceptions for ourselves: I know I shouldn't do X, but just this once, I will.

34. Even though we now have a better theoretical understanding of a categorical imperative, its actual existence has yet to be determined.

to it. In fact, the sublimity and inner dignity of the command in the duty are so much the more evident, the less subjective causes favor it and the more they oppose it, without being able to weaken the obligation of the law or to diminish its validity in the slightest.

Here, then, we see philosophy brought indeed to a difficult position, since it has to be firmly fixed, although nothing in heaven or earth supports it. Here it must show its purity as the self-sustaining author of its own laws, not the mouthpiece of those laws whispered to it by some implanted sense or who knows what immature nature. These may be better than nothing, yet they can never afford principles dictated by reason, whose source must be wholly a priori, hence their commanding authority that expects everything from the supremacy of the law and the due respect for it, and nothing from inclination, which condemns the human being to self-contempt and inward abhorrence.[35]

[426]

Not only is every empirical element quite incapable of contributing to the principle of morality, it is even highly disadvantageous to the purity of morals. The proper and inestimable worth of an absolutely good will consists precisely in this: The principle of action is free from all influence of contingent grounds that only experience can provide. We cannot too much or too often repeat our warning against this lazy, even sordid, way of thinking that seeks its principle in empirical motives and laws. Human reason in its weariness is glad to rest on this pillow and, in a dream of sweet illusions (where, instead of Juno, it embraces a cloud[36]), substitute for morality a bastard patched up from limbs of various origin that looks like anything one chooses to see in it, except virtue to one who has once beheld her in her true form.*

---

*To behold virtue in her proper form is nothing else but to contemplate morality stripped of all admixture of sensible things and of every spurious ornament of reward or self-love. How much virtue then eclipses everything else that appears charming to the

35. Kant is pointing out what a difficult position we are now in. The categorical imperative is an a priori principle that holds for all rational beings. We do not derive it from any empirical facts about human beings, nor do we necessarily follow it from any typical human motivations (because we can do our duty even when we do not want to).

36. This is a reference to ancient myth. Zeus tricked Ixion into embracing a cloud he had shaped as his wife, Hera (Juno in Roman myth), whom Ixion coveted.

The question, then, is this: "Is it a necessary law *for all rational beings* to always judge their actions by maxims that they can themselves will should serve as universal laws?" If so, then it must be connected (altogether a priori) with the very concept of the will of a rational being in general. But in order to discover this connection we must, however reluctantly, take a step into metaphysics, although a domain of it distinct from speculative philosophy, namely, the metaphysics of morals. In a practical philosophy, where we must ascertain not the grounds of what *happens*, but the laws of what *ought to happen*, even if it never does, i.e., objective practical laws, it is not necessary to inquire about the grounds of why anything pleases or displeases, how the pleasure of mere sensation differs from taste, and whether the latter is distinct from a general satisfaction of reason. Nor must we examine what feelings of pleasure or displeasure rest on and how desires and inclinations arise from these to produce maxims through the cooperation of reason. All this belongs to an empirical psychology, the second part of physics, regarded as the *philosophy of nature* insofar as it is based on *empirical laws*. But here we are concerned with objective practical laws and, consequently, with the relation of the will to itself to the extent it is determined by reason alone, in which case all references to anything empirical are necessarily excluded. If *reason of itself alone* determines the conduct (and it is this possibility we are now investigating), it must necessarily do so a priori.[37]

[427]

Represented as a faculty of determining itself to action in accordance with the *representation of certain laws*, the will, as such, can be found only in rational beings. Now, that which serves the will as the objective ground of its self-determination is the *end*, and, if assigned by reason alone, it must apply to all rational beings. On the other hand, that con-

---

affections, everyone may readily recognize with the least exertion of reason, if it is not wholly spoiled for abstraction.

37. Kant has arrived at this question because of the way the categorical imperative determines the will of all rational beings. How, in other words, can reason command all rational beings to do something independently of the other motives they might have?

taining merely the ground of possibility of the action whose effect is the end is called the *means*. The subjective ground of desire is the *incentive*, the objective ground of volition is the *motive*; hence the distinction between subjective ends, which rest on incentives, and objective ends, which depend on motives valid for every rational being. Practical principles are *formal* when they discount all subjective ends; they are *material* when they adopt these and therefore particular incentives to action. The ends that a rational being proposes arbitrarily as effects of its actions (material ends) are all just relative, for only their relation to a particular kind of faculty of desire of the subject gives them their worth.[38] This cannot therefore provide principles universal and necessary for all rational beings and for every volition, i.e., practical laws. Hence all these relative ends can give rise only to hypothetical imperatives.

[428]

Supposing, however, there were something *whose existence* had *in itself* an absolute worth, something which, being *an end in itself*, could be a ground of definite laws; then in this and in this alone would lie the ground of a possible categorical imperative, i.e., a practical law.

Now I say that human beings, and in general any rational being, *exist* as ends in themselves, *not merely as a means* to be arbitrarily used by this or that will; in all their actions, those that concern themselves or other rational beings, people must always be regarded *at the same time as an end*.[39] All objects of the inclinations have only a conditional worth, for if the inclinations and the needs founded on them did not exist, then their object would be without value. But the inclinations, themselves being sources of need, are so far from having an absolute worth for which they should be desired that complete freedom from them must be the universal wish of every rational being. Thus the worth of any object *which is to be acquired* by our action is always conditional. Beings whose existence depends not on our will but on nature have nevertheless, if they are irrational beings, only a relative value as means

38. The goals or purposes (in Kant's words, "ends") that rational beings set for themselves are usually particular to them—things that they want for themselves given their own desires and plans. As those ends are conditional, they cannot determine the will in a way consistent with the operation of the categorical imperative. In the subsequent paragraphs, Kant will try to determine what the proper end of the categorical imperative could be.

39. It sounds a bit strange to say that all rational beings are ends of moral action. Part of the issue here is with the English translation, but we can think about an end in different ways. Although they are not goals or purposes we're trying to accomplish, rational beings have unconditional value. This makes them the only type of end appropriate to the categorical imperative, which permits us to act only on those maxims we could will for all rational beings. But why? Because, as Kant explains in the following paragraphs, other rational beings are the objects of our respect.

and are therefore called *things*. Rational beings, by contrast, are called *persons*, because their very nature identifies them as ends in themselves, i.e., as something that must not be used merely as means and to that extent restricts* arbitrary choice (and is an object of respect). These beings, therefore, are not merely subjective ends whose existence has a worth *for us* as an effect of our action, but rather *objective ends*, i.e., things whose existence is an end in itself. Moreover, this is an end; no other end can substitute for it, to which it should serve *merely* as means. Otherwise, nothing at all would possess *absolute* worth. And if all worth were conditioned and therefore contingent, then there would be no supreme practical principle of reason whatsoever.

If, then, there is a supreme practical principle and, with respect to the human will, a categorical imperative, it must be a principle that, being drawn from the representation of that which is necessarily an end for everyone because it is *an end in itself*, constitutes an *objective* principle of will and can therefore serve as a universal practical law. The ground of this principle is that *rational nature exists as an end in itself*. Human beings necessarily conceive their own existence this way; and to that extent, it is a *subjective* principle of human actions. But every other rational being regards its existence in this way on the same rational ground also valid for me. It is thus at the same time an *objective* principle from which, as a supreme practical law, all laws of the will must be able to be derived. The practical imperative will therefore be as follows: *Act so as to treat humanity, whether in your own person or in the person of any other, always at the same time as an end, never merely as means.*[40] We will now inquire whether this can be accomplished.

[429]

---

*This proposition is stated here as a postulate. Its grounds will be found in the concluding section.

40. This is the first appearance of what will eventually be called the Formula of Humanity.

To stick with the previous examples:[41]

First, necessary duty to oneself: He who contemplates suicide should ask himself whether his action can be consistent with the idea of humanity *as an end in itself.* If he destroys himself to escape painful circumstances, he uses a person merely as *a means* to maintain a tolerable condition until death. But a man is not a thing, i.e., something that can be used *merely* as a means, but must in all his actions be considered an end in himself. I cannot, therefore, dispose in any way of a man in my own person so as to maim, damage, or kill him. (To avoid all misunderstanding, I omit the question of amputating limbs, for example, exposing my life to danger in order to preserve it, etc. Defining this principle more precisely belongs to ethics proper.)

Second, necessary or owed duties to others: He who is thinking about making a lying promise to others will see at once that he would be using another human being *merely as a means*, without the other person containing at the same time the end in himself. For he whom I propose to use by such a promise for my own purposes cannot possibly agree with

[430]   my mode of acting toward him and, therefore, cannot himself contain the end of this action. This violation of the principle of humanity in other human beings is more obvious if we consider examples of attacks on their freedom and property. Then it is clear that he who transgresses the rights of human beings intends to use the person of others merely as a means, without considering that as rational beings they ought always to be esteemed also as ends, i.e., beings who must be capable of containing in themselves the end of the very same action.*

---

*Let it not be thought that the common *quod tibi non vis fieri* [what you don't want to happen to yourself, don't do to another] could serve here as the standard or principle. For it is derived only from a principle, though with several limitations. It cannot be a universal law, for it does not contain the ground of duties to oneself, nor of the duties of

41. Kant is not changing his explanation of the previous examples. He is now showing how they are also consistent with the new claim he has just made (that rational beings are ends in themselves).

Third, contingent (meritorious) duties to oneself: It is not enough that the action does not conflict with humanity in our own person as an end in itself, it must also *harmonize with it*. Now humanity has capacities of greater perfection, which belong to the end of nature regarding humanity in our own person. To neglect these might be consistent perhaps with the *maintenance* of humanity as an end in itself, but not with its *advancement*.[42]

Fourth, meritorious duties toward others: The natural end of all human beings is their own happiness. Now humanity might indeed continue to exist, even if no one contributed anything to the happiness of others, provided he did not intentionally subtract anything from it. After all, this would only harmonize negatively, not positively, with *humanity as an end in itself*, if everyone does not also endeavor, as far as he is able, to further the ends of others. For the ends of any subject that is an end in himself must as far as possible be also *my* ends, if that representation is to have its *full* effect on me.

This principle, that humanity and in general every rational nature is *an end in itself* (the supreme limiting condition of every human being's [431] freedom of action), is not borrowed from experience: First, because it is universal, applying to all rational beings, about which experience is incapable of determining anything. Second, because this principle does not present humanity as an end of human beings (subjectively), i.e., an object human beings themselves actually adopt as an end, but rather as an objective end that must as a law constitute the supreme limiting condition of all our subjective ends, whatever our ends may be, it must arise

---

love to others. Many would gladly consent that others should not benefit them, provided only that they might be excused from showing benevolence to them. Nor in the end does that entail duties of strict obligation to one another, for on this ground the criminal might argue against the judge who punishes him, and so on.

42. In other words, treating yourself as an end requires more than merely not harming or "maintaining" yourself.

from pure reason. In fact, the *objective* ground of all practical legislation lies (according to the first principle) *in the rule* and its form of universality, which makes it capable of being a law (at least, for example, a law of nature). But the *subjective* principle is in the *end*. By the second principle, the subject of all ends is each rational being, inasmuch as it is an end in itself. Hence follows the third practical principle of the will, the ultimate condition of its harmony with universal practical reason, namely, the idea *of the will of every rational being as a universally legislative will.*[43]

On this principle, all maxims inconsistent with the will's universal legislation are rejected. Thus the will is not subject simply to the law, but subject so that it must be regarded *as* self-legislating, and, on this ground alone, subject to the law (of which it can regard itself the author).

In previous formulations—namely, those based on the concept of the lawfulness of actions, generally similar to an *order of nature*, and those based on the universal *preference* of rational beings as *ends* in themselves—these imperatives, precisely because they were represented as categorical, excluded from any share in their commanding authority all mixture of interest as an incentive. They were, however, only *assumed* to be categorical, because such an assumption was necessary to explain the concept of duty. But the existence of practical propositions that command categorically could not be proved independently, nor can it be proved in this section. One thing, however, could be done, namely, to indicate in the imperative itself, by some determinate expression, that all

[432]   interest is renounced in the case of willing from duty, the specific criterion of categorical, distinguished from hypothetical, imperatives. This is done in the present formulation of the principle, namely, in the idea of the will of every rational being as a *universally legislating will.*

Although a will *that is subject to laws* may be bound to this law by means of an interest, a will that is itself a supreme lawgiver, so far as it is such, cannot possibly depend on any interest, since a will so dependent

43. The first two practical principles are the categorical imperative (now referred to as the Formula of Universal Law) and the Formula of Humanity. Kant is now introducing the Formula of the Kingdom of Ends.

would still need another law restricting the interest of its self-love by the condition that it should be valid as universal law.

Thus the *principle* that every human will is *a will which in all its maxims gives universal laws,** provided it be otherwise justified, would be *very well adapted* to be the categorical imperative, in this respect, namely, that precisely because of the idea of universal legislation, it *is not based on interest,* and therefore, it alone among all possible imperatives can be *unconditional.* Or better yet, converting the proposition: If there is a categorical imperative (that is, a law for the will of every rational being), it can only command that everything be done from maxims of one's will regarded as such that could at the same time determine it should have itself as an object giving universal laws. For in that case, only the practical principle and the imperative it obeys are unconditional, since they cannot be grounded on any interest.[44]

Looking back now on all previous attempts to discover the principle of morality, we need not wonder why they all failed. It was seen that a human being is bound to laws by duty, but it was not observed that the laws to which he is subject are only those *of his own universal law-giving.* At the same time, they are *universal,* and he is only bound to act in conformity with his own will. This is a will designed by nature, however, to give universal laws. For when one has thought of human beings only as subject to a law (whatever it might be), then this law required some interest, either by way of attraction or constraint, since it did not originate as a law from *his own* will but was according to a law obliged by *something else* to act in a certain manner. Now by this necessary consequence, all the labor spent in finding a supreme principle of duty was irrevocably

[433]

---

*I may be excused from providing examples to elucidate this principle, since those that have already been used to elucidate the categorical imperative and its formula would serve for the similar purpose here.

44. In the previous few paragraphs, Kant clarifies his claims about the moral law and lawgiving, arguing that no other incentive than a respect for law determines a rational will that acts from duty. All rational beings are at the same time both lawgivers and law followers; there is no external source that issues moral commands.

lost. For people never found duty, but only a necessity of acting from a certain interest. Whether this interest was private or not, the imperative was conditional and certainly could not be capable of being a moral command. I will therefore call this the principle of **autonomy** of the will, in contrast with every other, which I accordingly count as **heteronomy**.[45]

The concept of the will of every rational being is one that must consider itself as giving universal laws through all the maxims of its will in order to judge itself and its actions from this point of view. This concept leads to another very fruitful concept dependent on it, namely, that *of a kingdom of ends*.

By a *kingdom*, I understand the union of different rational beings in a system through common laws. Since it is laws that determine the ends in accordance with their universal validity, if we abstract the personal differences of rational beings and likewise all content of their private ends, we are able to think of all ends combined in a systematic whole (including both rational beings as ends in themselves, and also the own ends that each may set for itself); that is to say, we can conceive a kingdom of ends possible on the preceding principles.

For all rational beings come under the law that each must treat itself and all others *never merely as means*, but in every case *at the same time as ends in themselves*. Thus results a systematic union of rational beings by common objective laws, a kingdom that may be called a kingdom of ends, since what these laws have in view is precisely the relation of these beings to one another as ends and as means. This is certainly only an ideal.[46]

[434]   A rational being belongs as a *member* to the kingdom of ends when, although giving universal laws in it, it is also itself subject to these laws. It belongs to it as *sovereign* when, while giving laws, it is not subject to the will of any other.

45. The distinction between autonomy and heteronomy is important for Kant because he wants to stress that we do not act from duty out of any incentive other than respect for the law. Acting from duty because we fear punishment, consider it prudent, or want other people to like us—these are all heteronomous. As Kant will eventually argue in Section 3, acting morally must be consistent with acting freely, and only autonomous willing can be free.

46. In other words, we are not trying to establish a literal kingdom of ends. This is a conceptual guide rather than an actual goal.

A rational being must always regard itself as giving laws either as a member or as sovereign in a kingdom of ends, rendered possible by the freedom of the will. It cannot, however, maintain the latter position merely by the maxims of its will, but only when it is a completely independent being without wants and with unrestricted power adequate to its will.

Morality, then, consists in the reference of all action to the legislation that alone can render a kingdom of ends possible. This legislation must be capable of being found in every rational being and of emanating from his will, so that the principle of this will is never to act on any maxim that could not also be a universal law and, accordingly, always to act such *that the will could at the same time regard itself as giving a universal law* through its maxims. If the maxims of rational beings are not by their own nature consistent with this objective principle, then the necessity of acting on it is called practical necessity, i.e., *duty*. Duty does not apply to the sovereign in the kingdom of ends, but it does to every member and to all in the same degree.[47]

The practical necessity of acting on this principle, that is, duty, does not rest at all on feelings, impulses, or inclinations, but solely on the relation of rational beings to one another, a relation in which the will of a rational being must always be regarded as *legislative*, since otherwise it could not be conceived as *an end in itself*. Reason, then, refers every maxim of the will, regarding it as legislating universally, to every other will and also to every action toward oneself. This is not on account of any other practical motive or any future advantage, but from the idea of the *dignity* of a rational being, obeying no law but that which it itself also gives.[48]

In the kingdom of ends everything has either *price* or *dignity*. Whatever has a price can be replaced by something else that is *equivalent*; in contrast, whatever is above all price, and therefore admits no equivalent, has a dignity.

47. We now see the importance of the universalizability of the categorical imperative. It is what allows us to make sure we act on maxims that are consistent with being a member of the kingdom of ends.

48. Kant's account of dignity is similar to contemporary conceptions of dignity. In Kant's terms, to say that rational beings are ends in themselves is to say that they are beings with dignity. They have an absolute value that should always be respected without exception.

[435] Whatever has reference to the general inclinations and wants of humankind has a *market price*; whatever, without presupposing a want, corresponds to a certain taste, i.e., a satisfaction in the mere purposeless play of our faculties, has an *affective price*; but that which constitutes the condition under which alone anything can be an end in itself does not have merely a relative worth, i.e., price, but an intrinsic worth, i.e., *dignity*.

Now morality is the condition under which alone a rational being can be an end in itself, since only through this is it possible that it should be a legislating member in the kingdom of ends. Thus morality, and humanity insofar as it is capable of morality, is that which alone has dignity. Skill and diligence in labor have a market price; wit, lively imagination, and moods have an affective price; in contrast, fidelity to promises and benevolence on the basis of principle (not from instinct) has an intrinsic worth.[49] Neither nature nor art contains any default substitute for these, for their worth consists not in the effects that arise from them, not in the use and advantage that they secure, but in the disposition of mind, i.e., the maxims of the will ready to manifest themselves in such actions, even though they would not have the desired effect. These actions also need no recommendation from any subjective disposition or taste so that they may be looked on with immediate favor and satisfaction; they need no immediate propensity or feeling for them. These actions exhibit the will that performs them as an object of an immediate respect, and nothing but reason is required to *impose* them on the will, not *flattery*, which, in the case of duties, would be a contradiction. This estimation therefore shows that the worth of such a way of thinking is dignity, situating it infinitely above all price, with which it cannot for a moment be placed in comparison or competition without violating its holiness.

49. Similar to the discussion about the good will from Section 1, Kant concludes that many human traits (e.g., wit and lively imagination) are nice to possess but not what makes rational beings intrinsically valuable. Rational beings
have dignity because of their moral capacities, the proper objects of respect.

What, then, justifies virtue or the morally good disposition in making such lofty claims? Nothing less than the privilege it secures to the rational being of participating *in the giving of universal laws* that qualifies him to be a member of a possible kingdom of ends. This is a privilege to which he was already destined by his own nature as being an end in itself and thereby legislating in the kingdom of ends. He is free from all natural laws, obeying only those he himself gives, and by which his maxims can belong to a system of universal law to which he at the same time submits himself. Nothing has any worth except what the law assigns it. The legislation itself that assigns the worth of everything must for that very reason possess dignity, i.e., an unconditional incomparable worth, and the word *respect* alone supplies a becoming expression for the esteem a rational being must have for it. *Autonomy*, then, is the ground of the dignity of human and of every rational nature.

[436]

The three ways of presenting the principle of morality are at root only so many formulas of the same law, one of which unites the other two in itself. These differ, but the difference is more subjectively than objectively practical, intended to bring an idea of reason nearer to intuition (by means of a certain analogy) and thereby nearer to feeling.[50] All maxims, in fact, have the following:

1. A *form*, consisting in universality, and in this view the formula of the moral imperative is expressed thus: that the maxims must be so chosen as if they were to serve as universal laws of nature.

2. A *matter*, namely, an end, and here the formula says that the rational being, as it is an end by its own nature and therefore an end in itself, must in every maxim serve as the condition limiting all merely relative and arbitrary ends.

50. The precise nature of the relationship between the three formulas presented here is the topic of some debate among Kant scholars. What Kant calls the "form" corresponds to the Formula of Universal Law (or the categorical imperative). What Kant calls the "matter" corresponds to the Formula of Humanity. What Kant calls the "complete determination" corresponds to the Formula of the Kingdom of Ends. In the subsequent paragraphs, Kant tries to tie all the things he has discussed in Section 2 together and explain how they relate to each other.

3. A *complete determination* of all maxims by means of that formula, namely, that all maxims ought by their own legislation harmonize with a possible kingdom of ends as with a kingdom of nature.*

There is a progression here through the categories of *unity* of the form of the will (its universality), *plurality* of the matter (the objects, i.e., the ends), and completeness and *totality* of the system of these. In forming our *judgment* of actions, it is always better to proceed with the strict method and take as ground the universal formula of the categorical

[437] imperative: *Act according to a maxim that can at the same time make itself a universal law.* If, however, we wish to gain access for the moral law, it is very useful to bring one and the same action under the three specified concepts and thereby, as far as possible, bring it nearer to intuition.

We can now end where we set out at the beginning, namely, with the concept of an unconditionally good will.[51] That *will is absolutely good* which cannot be evil, in other words, whose maxim, if made a universal law, could never contradict itself. This principle, then, is its supreme law: *Act always on such a maxim you can at the same time will to be a universal law.* This is the sole condition under which a will can never contradict itself, and such an imperative is categorical. Since the validity of the will as a universal law for possible actions is analogous to the universal connection of the existence of things by general laws, the formal aspect of nature in general, the categorical imperative can also be expressed thus: *Act in accordance with maxims that can at the same time have themselves as*

---

*Teleology considers nature as a kingdom of ends; ethics regards a possible kingdom of ends as a kingdom of nature. In the first case, the kingdom of ends is a theoretical idea, adopted to explain what actually is. In the latter case, it is a practical idea, adopted to bring about that which does not yet exist, but which can be realized by our conduct—namely, if it conforms to this idea.

51. This statement refers back to the beginning of Section 1.

universal laws of nature for their object. Such, then, is the formula of an absolutely good will.

Rational nature is distinguished from the rest of nature by setting an end for itself. This end would be the matter of every good will. The idea of a will that is absolutely good without being limited by any condition (of attaining this or that end) must be abstracted from all the ends to be *effected* (since otherwise this would make every will only relatively good). It follows that in this case the end must be conceived not as an end to be effected, but as a *self-sufficient* end. Consequently, it is conceived only negatively, i.e., as that which we must never act against and which, therefore, must never be regarded merely as means but in every volition must likewise be esteemed as an end. Now this end can be nothing but the subject of all possible ends, since this is also the subject of a possible absolutely good will. Such a will cannot without contradiction be subordinated to any other object. The principle—act in regard to every rational being (yourself and others) in such a way that your maxim is simultaneously always valid as an end in itself—is basically identical with the principle—act according to a maxim which, at the same time, involves its own universal validity for every rational being. In using means for every end, I should limit my maxims to the condition of holding as a law for every subject. This amounts to the same thing as the subject of ends, i.e., the rational being itself, being made the necessary ground of all maxims of action that should never be employed merely as means but as the supreme limiting condition restricting the use of all means, i.e., always and at the same time an end.

[438]

It follows incontestably that, whatever laws any rational being may be subject to, this being, as an end in itself, must also be able to regard itself as legislating universally with respect to these same laws, since it is precisely this fitness of the maxims for universal legislation that distinguishes it as an end in itself. It follows that this implies that its dignity

(prerogative) above all mere physical beings must always take its maxims from the point of view that regards itself and, likewise, every other rational being as law-giving beings (which is why they are also called persons). In this way, a world of rational beings (*mundus intelligibilis*) is possible as a kingdom of ends, by virtue of the legislation proper to all persons as its members. Therefore, every rational being must act as if it were by its maxims always a legislating member in the universal kingdom of ends. The formal principle of these maxims is this: Act as if your maxim were to serve at the same time as the universal law (of all rational beings). A kingdom of ends is thus only possible on the analogy of a kingdom of nature, the former, however, only by maxims, i.e., self-imposed rules, the latter, only by the laws of efficient causes acting under external necessity. Nevertheless, although the system of nature is looked upon as a machine, so far as it refers to rational beings as its ends, it is accorded on these grounds the name of a kingdom of nature. Such a kingdom of ends would actually be realized by means of maxims conforming to the rules the categorical imperative prescribes for all rational beings, *if they were universally followed*.[52]

But a rational being, even if it strictly follows this maxim itself, cannot count on similar obedience in others, nor, as a fit member, expect harmony with the kingdom of nature and its orderly arrangements. Thus forms a kingdom of ends to which he himself contributes and that favors his expectation of happiness, and thus the law: Act in accordance with maxims of a member legislating universal laws for a merely possible kingdom of ends remains in full force because it commands categorically. And in exactly this lies the paradox: The mere dignity of humanity as a rational creature, without any other end or advantage to be attained by it, in other words, respect for a mere idea, should yet serve as an inflexible precept of the will. Precisely in the maxim's independence from all such incentives, its sublimity consists and makes every rational subject

[439]

52. Here and on the previous page Kant is further explaining how the concepts he has introduced thus far fit together. The kingdom of ends incorporates most of what he has already explained.

worthy to be a legislative member in the kingdom of ends.[53] For otherwise it would have to be conceived only as subject to the physical law of its wants. Should we suppose the kingdom of nature and the kingdom of ends to be united under one sovereign so that the latter kingdom thereby ceased to be a mere idea and acquired true reality, then the sovereign, although undoubtedly gaining the addition of a strong incentive, would by no means increase its intrinsic worth. For this sole absolute lawgiver must, notwithstanding this, always be conceived as estimating the worth of rational beings only by their impartial behavior as prescribed to them from that idea [the dignity of humanity] alone. The essence of things is not altered by their external relations, and, not considering these, that which alone constitutes the absolute worth of a human being is also that by which he must be judged, whoever the judge may be and even by the Highest Being. *Morality*, then, is the relation of actions to the autonomy of the will, i.e., to the autonomy of potential universal legislation through its maxims. An action consistent with the autonomy of the will is *permitted*; one that does not agree is *forbidden*. A will whose maxims necessarily coincide with the laws of autonomy is a *holy* will, good absolutely. The dependence of a will not absolutely good on the principle of autonomy (moral necessity) is *obligation*. This cannot be applied, then, to a holy being. The objective necessity of actions from obligation is called *duty*.

[440]

From what has just been said, it is easy to see how it happens that, although the concept of duty implies subjection to the law, we still ascribe a certain *dignity* and sublimity to the person who fulfils all his duties. There is not, indeed, any sublimity in him, so far as he is *subject* to the moral law; but inasmuch as in regard to that very law he is likewise a *legislator*. On that account alone is he subject to the moral law and has sublimity. We have also shown that neither fear nor inclination, but simply respect for the law, is the incentive that can give actions a moral worth. The proper object of respect is our own will, so far as we suppose it

53. The capacity of rational beings to determine their wills by the moral law independently of any of their other incentives is, for Kant, intimately related to their dignity. We are self-legislating, a power that distinguishes us from other (what Kant calls "natural") beings whose wills are determined by their desires or instincts.

to act only under the condition that its maxims are potentially universal laws, which is ideally possible for us. And the dignity of humanity consists precisely in this capacity of being universally legislative, though with the condition that it is itself subject to this same legislation.

Autonomy of the Will[54]

Autonomy of the will is that property by which it is a law to itself (independently of any property of the objects of volition). The principle of autonomy, then, is this: Never choose otherwise than that the same volition shall comprehend the maxims of our choice as a universal law. We cannot prove that this practical rule is an imperative, i.e., that the will of every rational being is necessarily bound to it as a condition, by a mere analysis of the concepts that occur in it, since it is a synthetic proposition. We must advance beyond the cognition of the objects to a critical examination of the subject, i.e., of pure practical reason, because this synthetic proposition, which commands apodictically, must be capable of being known wholly a priori. This matter, however, does not belong to the present section. That this principle of autonomy in question is the sole principle of morals can readily be shown by mere analysis of the concepts of morality. In this analysis, we find that its principle must be a categorical imperative and that what this commands is neither more nor less than this very autonomy.

Heteronomy of the Will[55]

[441]   If the will seeks the law to determine it *anywhere else* than in the fitness of its maxims to be universal laws, i.e., if it goes beyond itself and seeks this law in the character of any of its objects, *heteronomy* always results. The will in that case does not give itself the law, but it is given by the object through its relation to the will. This relation, whether it rests on inclination or on representations of reason, only admits hypothetical

54. Autonomy is something of a specialized term for Kant. An autonomous person is someone who self-governs by making the moral law the guiding principle of her will.

55. Heteronomy is the contrast to autonomy.

imperatives: I ought to do something *because I wish for something else.* By contrast, the moral, and therefore the categorical, imperative says: I ought to do so and so, even though I did not wish for anything else. For example, the former says: I ought not to lie, if I want to retain my reputation; whereas the latter says: I ought not to lie, although it would bring no shame on me. The latter therefore must so far abstract from all objects that they shall have no *influence* on the will, in order that practical reason (will) may not be restricted to administering the interests of others, and not belonging to it, but may simply prove its own commanding authority as the supreme legislation. Thus, for example, I ought to try to promote the happiness of others, not as if its existence mattered to me (whether by immediate inclination or any satisfaction indirectly gained through reason), but simply because the maxim that excludes the happiness of others cannot be comprehended as a universal law in one and the same volition.

DIVISION OF ALL PRINCIPLES OF MORALITY FROM THE ASSUMED FUNDAMENTAL CONCEPT OF HETERONOMY

Here, as elsewhere, human reason in its pure use, so long as it has not been critically examined, has first tried all possible wrong ways before it succeeded in finding the one true way.[56]

All principles that can be taken from this point of view are either *empirical* or *rational.* The *former*, drawn from the principle of *happiness*, [442] are built on physical or moral feelings; the *latter*, drawn from the principle of *perfection*, are built on either the rational concept of perfection as a possible effect or that of an independent perfection (the will of God) as the determining cause of our will.[57]

Empirical principles are wholly incapable of serving as a foundation for moral laws. The universality with which these should hold for all rational beings without distinction, the unconditional practical necessity thereby imposed on them, is lost when the ground is derived from the

56. This is a reference to the *Critique of Pure Reason*, Kant's earlier work on theoretical reason. In the following paragraphs, Kant articulates some of the incorrect principles of morality that other people have proposed—namely, principles based on happiness and on perfection.

57. In this section, Kant will try to show that other possible principles cannot be the source of morality. He discusses happiness and perfection.

particular constitution of human nature or the accidental circumstances in which it is placed. The principle of *one's own happiness*, however, is the most objectionable, not merely because it is false, and experience contradicts the supposition that prosperity is always proportional to good conduct, nor merely because it contributes nothing to the establishment of morality, since it is quite a different thing to make a human being prosperous rather than good, or to make one prudent and sharp-sighted for his own advantage rather than virtuous. This is because its incentives for morality are such as to undermine it and destroy its sublimity, since they put the motives for virtue and vice in the same class and teach us only to make a better calculation, the specific difference between virtue and vice being entirely extinguished. (On the other hand, as to moral feeling, this supposed special sense,* the appeal to it is indeed superficial when those who cannot *think* believe that *feeling* will help them out, even concerning general laws; and besides, feelings, which naturally differ infinitely in degree, cannot furnish a uniform standard of good and evil, nor has anyone a right to form judgments for others by his own feelings.) Nevertheless, this moral feeling is closer to morality and its dignity in the respect that it honors virtue by *immediately* bestowing our satisfaction and esteem on it and does not, as it were, tell it to its face that we are not attached to it by its beauty but rather by our advantage.

[443]

Among the *rational* principles of morality, the ontological concept of *perfection*, notwithstanding its defects, is better than the theological

---

*I count the principle of moral feeling under that of happiness, because every empirical interest promises to contribute to our welfare through the agreeableness that a thing affords, whether it be immediately and without a view to profit, or whether profit be considered. We must likewise, with *Francis Hutcheson* [Hutcheson (1694–1746) was a Scottish sentimentalist], classify the principle of sympathy with the happiness of others under his assumed moral sense.

concept that derives morality from a Divine absolutely perfect will.[58] The former is, no doubt, empty and indefinite and consequently useless for finding within the boundless field of possible reality the greatest amount suitable for us. Moreover, in attempting to specifically distinguish the reality of which we are now speaking from all others, it inevitably tends to turn in a circle and cannot avoid tacitly presupposing the morality that it is to explain. It is nevertheless preferable to the theological view, first, because we have no intuition of the divine perfection and can only deduce it from our own concepts, the foremost of which is morality. Our explanation would thus involve a crude circle. Subsequently, if we avoid this, the only concept of the Divine will remaining to us is a concept made up of the attributes of the desire for glory and domination, combined with the frightening representations of might and vengeance. Any system of morals erected on this groundwork would be directly opposed to morality.

If I had to choose between the concept of the moral sense and that of perfection in general, however (two systems that, if nothing else, do not weaken morality, although they are totally incapable of serving as its groundwork), then I should opt for the latter, because it at least withdraws the decision of the question from sensibility and brings it to the court of pure reason. Although even here it decides nothing, in any case it preserves the indefinite idea (of a will good in itself) unfalsified until it shall be more precisely defined.

For the rest, I think I may be excused here from a wide-ranging refutation of all these doctrines. That would only be superfluous labor, since it is so easy and probably so well understood even by those whose role requires them to support one of these theories (because their audience would not tolerate delay of judgment). But what interests us more here is to know that the prime ground of morality laid down by all these

58. Here Kant claims that we might try to derive morality from the concept of perfection itself, contrasting it to the idea of God's perfection. Kant considers neither of these avenues promising, although he thinks the concept of perfection itself has fewer problems than God's perfection.

principles is nothing but heteronomy of the will, and for this reason, they must necessarily miss their target.[59]

[444] In every case where an object of the will has to be taken as the ground in order to prescribe the rule determining that will, there the rule is simply heteronomy. The imperative is conditional, namely, *if* or *because* one wishes for this object, one should act so and so; hence it can never command morally, i.e., categorically. Whether the object determines the will by means of inclination, as in the principle of one's own happiness, or by means of reason directed to objects of our possible volition generally, as in the principle of perfection, in either case the will never determines itself *immediately* by the concept of the action, but only by the incentives of the foreseen effect of the action on the will. *I ought to do something, on this account, because I wish for something else.* Here there must be yet another law in me as its ground, by which I necessarily will this other thing, and this law again requires an imperative to restrict this maxim. The impulse that the representation of an object within the reach of our faculties can exercise on the will of the subject, as a result of its natural constitution, belongs to the nature of the subject, whether sensibility (inclination and taste) or the understanding and reason, whose employment on an object is, by the peculiar constitution of their natures, exercised with satisfaction. It follows that the law would be, properly speaking, given by nature, and, as such, it must be known and proved by experience and would consequently be contingent and therefore incapable of being an apodictic practical rule, such as the moral rule must be. Not only so, but it is *inevitably only heteronomy*; the will does not give itself the law but is given it by an extraneous impulse through a particular natural constitution of the subject adapted to receive it.[60]

An absolutely good will, then, the principle of which must be a categorical imperative, will be indeterminate regarding all objects and will contain merely the *form of volition* generally, and that as autonomy,

59. Rather than itemize the other incorrect possibilities for the derivation of morality, Kant simply groups them all together under the broad heading of principles grounded on heteronomy.

60. According to Kant, whatever principles we try to derive from any heteronomous morality will be merely conditional. If, for example, we claim that morality derives from our desire to be well liked, the principles we try to derive will hold only for people who have this desire. Additionally, Kant thinks we can pose the question: Why should I want to be well liked? Morality grounded on this desire cannot by itself answer this question.

i.e., the capability of the maxims of every good will to make themselves a universal law, which is itself the only law that the will of every rational being imposes on itself, without needing to assume any incentive or interest as a foundation.

How such a synthetic practical a priori proposition is possible, and why it is necessary, is a problem whose solution does not lie within the bounds of the metaphysics of morals. We have not here asserted its truth, much [445] less professed to have a proof of it in our power. We simply showed by the development of the universally received concept of morality that an autonomy of the will is inevitably connected with it or, rather, is its ground. Whoever, then, holds morality to be anything real, and not a chimerical idea without any truth, must likewise accept the principle of it assigned here. This section, therefore, like the first, was merely analytical. Now to prove that morality is no figment of the imagination, which it cannot be if the categorical imperative and with it the autonomy of the will is true, and as an a priori principle absolutely necessary, supposes the *possibility of a synthetic use of pure practical reason*, which, however, we cannot explore without first providing a *critical* examination of this faculty of reason. In the concluding section, we shall present the principal outlines of this critical examination sufficient for our purpose.[61]

61. Kant wants to be clear about what he has accomplished in this section. He has established only what a synthetic a priori moral principle would look like. He has not established that it is possible for human beings to follow it, which is the task he takes up in Section 3.

Transition from the Metaphysics of Morals to the Critique of Pure Practical Reason

THE CONCEPT OF FREEDOM IS THE KEY THAT EXPLAINS THE AUTONOMY OF THE WILL

[446]   THE *WILL* IS A KIND OF CAUSALITY OF LIVING BEINGS IN SO FAR AS THEY are rational; and *freedom* would be the characteristic of such causality, allowing it to be efficient independent of external causes *determining* it.[1] Similarly, *physical necessity* is the characteristic of causality of all irrational beings that determines their activity by the influence of external causes.

This definition of freedom is *negative* and thus unfruitful for the discovery of its essence, but it leads to a *positive* conception that is fuller and more productive,[2] since the concept of causality involves that of laws, according to which something we call a cause must be supposed to entail something else, the effect.[3] Although not a property of the will dependent on physical laws, freedom is not lawless. On the contrary, it must be a causality acting according to unchanging laws, but of a particular kind. Otherwise, free will would be an absurdity. Natural necessity is a heteronomy of efficient causes, for every effect is possible only according to the law that something else determines that an efficient cause will exercise its

1. Recall from the previous section that a rational will is self-determining: Rational creatures decide on what basis they will act. According to Kant, this would make freedom (rather than, for example, instinct) the "causality" of the rational will.

2. The definition is negative because it only tells you what freedom of the will is not (e.g., the will is not determined by "external causes") rather than telling you what freedom of the will is.

3. Kant has an extended discussion of the nature of causality in the *Critique of Pure Reason*, so some of the claims he makes here draw on that work.

[447]   causality.[4] What else can freedom of the will be but autonomy, i.e., the property of the will to be a law unto itself? The proposition that the will is in every action a law unto itself expresses this principle only: to act on no other maxim than having an object itself as a universal law. Now this is precisely the formula of the categorical imperative and the principle of morality, so that a free will and a will subject to moral laws are one and the same.[5]

If the freedom of the will is presupposed, morality, together with its principle, follows from it by mere analysis of the concept. However, the latter[6] is a synthetic proposition. An absolutely good will is one whose maxim can always be regarded as a universal law. This property of its maxim can never be discovered by analyzing the concept of an absolutely good will. Such synthetic propositions are only possible when two cognitions are connected by their union with a third in which they are both to be found. The *positive* concept of freedom furnishes this third cognition. In contrast to physical causes, this cannot be in the nature of the sensible world (in which the concept of something related as cause to *something else* as effect is conjoined). We cannot now directly show the third thing to which freedom points us, and of which we have an idea a priori. Nor can we yet explain how the concept of freedom is shown to be legitimate from principles of pure practical reason, and with it the possibility of a categorical imperative. Further preparation is required.[7]

Freedom Must Be Presupposed as a Property of the Will of All Rational Beings

It is not enough to attribute freedom to our will, no matter the reason. We must have sufficient grounds for ascribing freedom to all rational beings. Morality serves as a law for us only because we are *rational beings*, and so it must be valid for all rational beings. As morality must be derived solely from the property of freedom, freedom must also be demonstrated

4. This is Kant's overly complicated way of saying that nature works according to causal laws. In other words, rocks don't move themselves; something else must cause them to move.

5. In this paragraph, Kant is resisting the idea that a free will would be one that does not operate according to laws at all. Instead, he wants to argue that a free will operates according to a special kind of law—namely, the moral law that he has just tried to describe in Section 2.
6. "The latter" refers to the phrase "its principle"—that is, the categorical imperative.

7. Recall from the end of Section 2 that Kant's task in this section is to show how a synthetic a priori moral principle is possible. Here he is pointing out that we cannot merely assume the existence of freedom of the will that he has just described in the previous paragraphs.

[448] to be a property of the will of all rational beings. It is insufficient, then, to prove freedom from certain supposed experiences of human nature. (That is quite impossible, as this can only be shown a priori.) Rather, we must demonstrate that it belongs to the activity of all rational beings endowed with a will. Now I say: Any being that can act only *under the idea of freedom* is for that very reason, from a practical point of view, really free.[8] In other words, all laws inseparably bound with freedom are valid for a rational being, as if his will had been revealed to be free in itself and in a way that is valid in theoretical philosophy.* I maintain that we must grant to every rational being with a will the idea of freedom, under which it acts entirely. In such a being, we conceive a reason that is practical; it has causality in reference to its objects. We cannot possibly conceive a reason whose judgments were consciously steered from any other quarter, for then the subject would ascribe the determination of its judgment not to its own reason, but rather to an impulse. It must regard itself as the author of its principles, independent of external influences. Consequently, as practical reason or as the will of a rational being, it must regard itself as free. In other words, the will of such a being can only be a will of its own if under the idea of freedom. This idea must therefore, from a practical point of view, be ascribed to every rational being.[9]

OF THE INTEREST ATTACHED TO THE IDEAS OF MORALITY

We have ultimately traced the definite concept of morality to the idea of freedom. We could not, however, prove this latter idea to be something

---

*I adopt this method of assuming freedom only *as an idea* that rational beings suppose in their actions so as to avoid the necessity of proving it in its theoretical aspect. The former is sufficient for my purpose. Even though the speculative proof has not been worked out, a being that can act only with the idea of freedom is bound by the same laws that would oblige a being who is actually free. Thus, we can escape the burden that weighs upon theory.

8. Acting "under the idea of freedom" is something of a technical term for Kant. (We can see this from his own footnote in this paragraph.) Kant's notion of an idea is derived from a lengthy and complex discussion in the *Critique of Pure Reason*. Without getting too ensnared in difficult interpretive questions, we can view an idea as a concept that has a regulative or sense-making role in the mind and in the actions of rational creatures. According to Kant, rational creatures can only make sense of themselves and their existence in the world by assuming that they are free. Kant will return to this claim in slightly more detail as the section progresses.

9. To get a clearer sense of what Kant means here, consider the following line of thought: Rational creatures deliberate about what to do, and they act based on those deliberations. (This is what Kant means by "practical reason.") This activity is, in Kant's view, a central characteristic of rationality. Now if the will is not free, that means that this activity is all for naught: Although we think we are deliberating and acting in light of those deliberations, something else external to that activity actually causes us to act. Yet, as Kant points out, there is no way for me as a rational creature to act while at the same time also believing that I am not the cause of my actions. I only know how to act one way—namely, by deliberating and deciding what to do. I do not know what it means to act without also assuming that I am the one causing my own actions.

[449]   actual in ourselves or in human nature. We only saw that it must be presupposed if we would conceive a being as rational and conscious of its causality in respect of its actions, i.e., endowed with a will. And so on the same grounds, we must attribute to every being endowed with reason and will the property of determining itself to actions under the idea of its freedom.

By presupposing this idea of freedom, we became aware of the law that the subjective principles of action, i.e., maxims, must always be assumed in such a way that they can also hold as objective, i.e., universal principles. They thus serve as universal laws by virtue of our own law-giving. But why, then, should I subject myself to this principle, simply as a rational being, thus also subjecting all other beings endowed with reason to it? I will concede that no interest *urges* me to this, as that would not yield a categorical imperative. I must *take* an interest in it and discern how this comes to pass; for this "ought" is actually a volition, valid for every rational being, provided only that reason, without any obstacles, would be practical. But beings like us are also affected by incentives of a different kind, namely, by sensibility, in which case reason does not always do what reason alone would do. For these beings, necessity is expressed only as an ought, because the subjective and the objective necessity differ.[10]

It seems as though the moral law, the principle of autonomy of the will, was only presupposed in the idea of freedom, as though we could not independently prove its reality and objective necessity. In that case, we should still have gained something considerable by at least determining the genuine principle more exactly than previous determinations. But regarding its validity and the practical necessity of subjecting oneself to it, we would not have advanced a step. If asked why the universal validity of our maxim as a law must be the condition restricting our actions, and on what we base the worth we assign to this manner

10. In this and the subsequent paragraphs, Kant is taking stock of where he has arrived in his argument. Although he has articulated and described the moral law (in Section 2) and has now suggested that freedom of the will is closely related to the moral law, there is much he has not yet established. Why, for example, do we experience the categorical imperative as binding in a way that is different from our other incentives?

of acting, we would respond, it is a worth so great that there can be no higher interest. And if asked further how by this alone a human being feels his own personal worth—in comparison with which an agreeable or disagreeable condition is to be regarded as nothing—to these questions, we could give no satisfactory answer.

[450]

We sometimes find that we can indeed take an interest in a personal quality, which does not involve any interest at all in the condition itself, provided that the former makes us capable of participating in the latter, in the event that reason was to bring about this distribution. In other words, merely being worthy of happiness can be of interest in itself, even without the motive of participating in this happiness. This judgment, however, is in fact only the effect of the importance of the moral law, which we presupposed (when we detach ourselves from every empirical interest by the idea of freedom). But we are not able to discern whether we ought to consider ourselves free in action and yet subject ourselves to certain laws. If we could, we could find a worth simply in our own person that can compensate us for the loss of everything that gives worth to our condition, but we cannot see how this is possible, and hence we cannot see how *the moral law derives its obligation.*

It must be freely admitted that a sort of circle is displayed here from which it seems impossible to escape. In the order of efficient causes, we assume that we are free, so that we can think of ourselves as subject to moral laws in the order of ends. And we subsequently conceive ourselves as subject to these laws, because we have attributed to ourselves freedom of the will. Freedom and self-legislation of the will are both autonomy and thus reciprocal concepts. For this very reason, the one must not be used to explain the other or to provide its foundation.[11] At most, logical purposes reduce apparently different representations of the same object to one single concept (as we reduce different fractions of the same value to the lowest common denominator).

11. The supposed circle here is that the moral law seems to be defined in terms of our freedom, and yet our freedom seems to be defined in terms of the moral law. Kant scholars disagree about whether this circle poses a genuine problem.

One way of inquiry remains, namely, to seek whether we take one perspective when, by means of freedom, we think ourselves as a priori efficient causes, and another point of view when we represent ourselves in accordance with our actions as effects we see before our eyes.

No subtle reflection is needed to make the following observation: We may well assume it to be a product of the most common under-[451] standing, even if it happens through an obscure feature of the faculty of judgment that it calls feeling. All the representations that come to us involuntarily (like those of the senses) do not enable us to know objects except by how they affect us. What they may be in themselves remains unknown.[12] With representations of this kind, even when applying the most strenuous attention and clarity of understanding, we can attain only the knowledge of *appearances*, never that of *things in themselves*. As soon as this distinction emerges (perhaps merely as a consequence of the difference observed between the representations given us from without, in which we are passive, and those we produce from ourselves, in which we are active), it follows that we must admit and assume something else behind the appearances that is not an appearance, namely, things in themselves, even if by ourselves we are satisfied that we can neither get nearer to them, as they can never be known to us except as they affect us, nor ever know what they are in themselves. This must yield a distinction, however crude, between a *world of sense* and the *world of understanding*, of which the former may vary according to differences in sensibility of many ways of contemplating the world, while the latter, on which it is grounded, always remains the same. Even with respect to himself, a person cannot pretend to know what he is in himself from knowledge acquired by internal sensation. As he does not, so to speak, create himself, and does not come by the concept of himself a priori but empirically, it naturally follows that he can obtain his knowledge even of himself only by his inner sense and, consequently, only through the appearances of

12. This discussion of perception of objects and the other remarks in this paragraph rely on arguments that Kant presents in the *Critique of Pure Reason*. There Kant claims that we can take up two "perspectives" when asking what we know about objects that exist independently from us: We can think of an object the way it appears to us—as an object that exists in space and time as represented to us by sensation. We can also think of an object as it exists independently of how it appears to us—what it is like "out there," so to speak, regardless of how we might encounter it. As Kant will explain, the problem is that we cannot know what objects are like independently from how we encounter them (how they are as "things in themselves"). Nonetheless, according to Kant, we still assume that there is something "out there" that causes objects to appear to us the way they do even if we cannot know what exactly that something is. This distinction Kant draws is known as the phenomenal/noumenal distinction. Phenomenal is how objects appear to us, while noumenal is how they are as things in themselves.

his nature and the way in which his consciousness is affected. At the same time, beyond the constitution of his own subject, made up of mere appearances, he must necessarily suppose something else as their ground, namely, his *ego*, whatever its constitution in itself may be. Thus, in respect to mere perception and receptivity of sensations, he must count himself as belonging to the *world of sense*. Regarding whatever there may be of pure activity in him (that which reaches consciousness immediately and not through the affected senses), he must count himself as belonging to the *intellectual world*, of which, however, he has no further knowledge.[13]

[452] A reflective human being must come to such a conclusion about all things that can be presented to him. This conclusion will probably be encountered even in persons of the most common understanding, who, as is well known, are very much inclined to suppose something else invisible and acting of itself behind the objects of the senses. But such understanding spoils all this by making the invisible sensible again; in other words, by wanting to render the invisible an object of intuition, they do not become at all the wiser.[14]

Now a person really finds in himself a faculty by which he distinguishes himself from everything else, even from himself as he is affected by objects, and that faculty is *reason*. As pure self-activity, this is elevated even above the *understanding*. For although the understanding is a self-activity and does not, like sense, merely contain representations that arise only when we are affected by things (and are therefore passive), it cannot produce from its own activity any concepts other than those that merely serve *to bring the sensible representations under rules* and thereby unite them in one consciousness. Without this use of sensibility, the understanding could not think at all. In contrast, reason shows such a pure self-activity under the name of ideas that it thereby far transcends everything that sensibility can supply. Reason thus exhibits its most important function in distinguishing the world

13. Just as we can think of objects as both (a) phenomenal, how we experience them, and (b) noumenal or "out there," independent of how we experience them, Kant claims that we also think of ourselves in this dual way: existing as embodied creatures in the world along with all other physical things and existing beyond embodiment as an intellect unlike other physical things. As in the case of objects, we cannot know exactly what our noumenal selves are or are like. We simply assume we have them.

14. Readers may find it difficult to believe that any "common understanding" would arrive at the phenomenal/noumenal distinction. Then again, it's very common for people to believe that humans have immaterial souls or for people to believe in ghosts. It's not unusual for people to think about themselves as some combination of body and mind, body and soul, or body and spirit.

of sense from that of understanding, thereby prescribing the limits of the understanding itself.[15]

On account of this, a rational being must regard itself as an intelligence (thus not from the side of its lower powers), as belonging to the world of understanding rather than sense. Thus a rational being has two standpoints from which it can regard itself and recognize laws governing the exercise of its powers and consequently all its actions. *First*, in so far as it belongs to the world of sense, it finds itself subject to laws of nature (heteronomy); *second*, it belongs to the intelligible world, under laws which, being independent of nature, are grounded not in experience, but in reason alone.

As a rational being, and consequently belonging to the intelligible world, a human being can never conceive the causality of his own will except on condition of the idea of freedom. Independence of the determinate causes of the sensible world (an independence that reason must always ascribe to itself) is freedom. The idea of freedom is inseparably connected with the concept of *autonomy*. And this in turn is connected with the universal principle of morality, which, as idea, is the ground of all actions of *rational* beings, just as the law of nature is the ground of all appearances.

[453]

Now we have removed the suspicion raised earlier, that a hidden circle was involved in our conclusion, moving from freedom to autonomy and from this to the moral law, namely, that we perhaps laid down the idea of freedom because of the moral law simply to infer in turn the latter from freedom. Consequently, it was charged that we could not offer any ground for this law but could present it only as a circular begging of the question, which well-disposed souls would gladly concede to us but which we could never put forward as a provable proposition. For now we see that when we conceive of ourselves as free, we transfer ourselves into the world of understanding as members of it. And we

15. The definitions of reason, sense, and understanding that appear in this paragraph are all derived from the *Critique of Pure Reason*.

also recognize the autonomy of the will with its consequence, morality. If we conceive of ourselves as under obligation, however, we consider ourselves as belonging to both the world of sense and at the same time the world of understanding.[16]

How Is a Categorical Imperative Possible?

The rational being, to the extent that it counts itself as intelligent, considers itself as belonging to the world of understanding. It is simply as an efficient cause belonging to that world that it calls its causality a *will*. On the other hand, it is also conscious of itself as a part of the world of sense, in which its actions, mere appearances of that causality, are displayed. We cannot, however, discern how they are possible from this causality we do not know. Instead, we must view these actions, belonging to the sensible world, as determined by other appearances, namely, desires and inclinations. If, therefore, I were only a member of the world of understanding, then all my actions would perfectly conform to the principle of autonomy of the pure will. If I were only a part of the world of sense, presumably my actions would necessarily conform wholly to the natural law of desires and inclinations, in other words, to the heteronomy of nature. (The former would rest on morality as the supreme principle, the latter on happiness.) However, *the world of understanding contains the ground of the world of sense, and consequently also of its laws*, and accordingly confers the law on my will immediately, which belongs wholly to the world of understanding and must be conceived as such. It follows, then, that on the one side, I must regard myself as a being belonging to the world of sense, yet on the other side, I must recognize that as an intelligence I am

[454] subject to the law of the world of understanding, i.e., to reason, which contains this law in the idea of freedom, and therefore, I am subject to the autonomy of the will. Consequently, I must regard the laws of the

16. We can see now why Kant thinks freedom and morality are closely connected. We are motivated to do our duty by reason alone and no other incentive. Our capacity for practical reason requires that we see ourselves as intellects not bound by the normal causality we find in the sensible world. We thus have the ability to obligate ourselves to the moral law by being both a free intellect and an embodied being.

world of understanding as imperatives for me and the actions conforming to them as duties.

And thus what makes categorical imperatives possible is this: The idea of freedom makes me a member of an intelligible world and, consequently, if I were nothing else, all my actions *would* always conform to the autonomy of the will. But as I at the same time intuit myself as a member of the world of sense, my actions *ought* so to conform. This *categorical ought* implies a synthetic a priori proposition: In addition to my will as affected by sensible desires, there is the idea of the same will belonging to the world of the understanding, pure and practical of itself, which contains the supreme condition of the same will according to reason. Precisely as to the intuitions of sense, there are the added concepts of the understanding, which of themselves signify nothing but lawful form in general. In this way, synthetic a priori propositions become possible, on which all knowledge of physical nature rests.[17]

The practical use of common human reason confirms the correctness of this deduction. There is no one, not even the most malicious villain, provided only he is otherwise accustomed to the use of reason, who, when we set before him examples of honesty of purpose, of steadfastness in following good maxims, of sympathy and general benevolence (even combined with great sacrifices of advantage and comfort), there is no one who does not wish that he might also possess these qualities. He cannot, on account of his inclinations and impulses, attain this in himself but wishes at the same time to be free from such burdensome inclinations. He proves by this that a will free from the impulses of sensibility transfers himself in thought into an order of things wholly different from that of his desires in the field of sensibility. He cannot expect to obtain by that wish any gratification of his desires, nor any condition that would satisfy any of his actual or supposed inclinations. This would forfeit the preeminence of the very idea

[455]

17. Kant believes he has now shown how the moral law is possible as a synthetic a priori proposition by showing how we can govern ourselves with it as both intelligible and sensible selves.

that elicits that wish from him. He can expect only a greater intrinsic worth of his own person. He believes himself to be this better person, however, when he transfers himself to the point of view of a member of the world of the understanding, as he is involuntarily forced to by the idea of freedom, of independence from *determining* causes of the world of sense. From this point of view, he is conscious of a good will, which by his own confession constitutes the law for the bad will he possesses as a member of the world of sense. This is a law whose authority he recognizes while transgressing it. What he morally "ought" to do is, then, his own necessary volition, as a member of the intelligible world. He thinks this as an "ought" only inasmuch as he likewise considers himself a member of the world of sense.[18]

Of the Extreme Limits of All Practical Philosophy

All people think of themselves as free in terms of the will. Hence all judgments about actions come as if they *ought to have happened*, even though they *have not happened*. This freedom is not a concept of experience, nor can it be so. Freedom still remains, even though experience exhibits the opposite of those requirements represented as necessary under the presupposition of freedom. On the other hand, it is equally necessary that everything that happens should be determined without any exception according to the laws of nature. This necessity of nature is likewise not an empirical concept, precisely because it involves the concept of necessity and consequently a priori cognition. But experience confirms this concept of nature, which must inevitably be presupposed if experience itself is to be possible, i.e., a connected knowledge of the objects of sense resting on general laws. Therefore, freedom is only an *idea* of reason, whose objective reality in itself is doubtful.[19] Nature is a *concept* of the *understanding* that proves, and must necessarily prove, its reality by examples from experience.

18. Again, it may seem counterintuitive that "common human reason" will reach Kant's conclusions, but we can see what he means with this example. A bad person can and does desire to be better. The ability to have this wish requires that this person is able to see other possible ways he could be. He must be able to occupy a perspective from which he judges that all his current desires and motivations are flawed. That perspective is the free intellect that grasps the moral law and is motivated by it.

19. This remark about an idea of reason is related to Kant's previous comments about acting under an idea of freedom (see note 8). Here an idea of reason is a kind of perfect example or archetype of something that we do not gain from experience. We cannot prove or demonstrate that freedom exists in the same way we could prove that, say, sea turtles or a molecule exist. Nonetheless, reason leads us to think about ideas, and they sometimes (as in the case of the idea of freedom) play a practical role in our lives.

From this arises a dialectic of reason, since the freedom attributed to the will appears to contradict the necessity of nature.[20] At this fork in the road, reason for *speculative purposes* finds the road of physical necessity a much more beaten and useful path than that of freedom. Yet for *practical purposes*, the narrow footpath of freedom is the only one that allows us to make use of reason in our conduct. It is equally impossible for the most subtle philosophy and the most common reason to rationalize away freedom. Philosophy must, then, assume that no real contradiction will be discovered between freedom and the natural necessity of precisely the same human actions, for it cannot give up the concept of nature any more than that of freedom.

[456]

Even though we would never be able to conceive how freedom is possible, we must at least remove this apparent contradiction in a convincing manner. If the thought of freedom either contradicts itself or is contrary to nature, then freedom, as opposed to natural necessity, would have to be entirely abandoned.

It is, however, impossible to escape this contradiction if the subject, which imagines itself free, thinks itself *in the same sense* or *in the same relation* when it calls itself free as when it regards the same action as subject to the law of nature. This is an unavoidable task of speculative philosophy, to show that its illusion respecting this contradiction rests on the fact that we think of a human being in a different sense and relation when we call him free than when we regard him as a part of nature subject to its laws. Speculative philosophy must therefore show that not only *can* both of these coexist very well, but that both must be viewed *as necessarily united* in the same subject. Otherwise, no support could be presented as to why we should burden reason with an idea that, although it may possibly *without contradiction* be united with another sufficiently established idea, still entangles us in a perplexity that puts reason in a tight spot about its theoretical employment. This duty,

20. The dialectic that arises here is an internal conflict between theoretical and practical reason. Theoretical reason wants to know or prove that free will exists or does not exist. Practical reason has to simply assume that we are free so that we can act.

however, belongs only to speculative philosophy to clear the way for practical philosophy.[21] The philosopher has no choice about whether to remove or leave untouched the apparent contradiction. In the latter case, the theory would be a *bonum vacans*, an empty good, where the fatalist would have cause to enter into possession of it, chasing out all morality that occupied its supposed domain without any title to it.

We cannot yet say that this is where the boundaries of practical philosophy begin. The settlement of that controversy does not belong to practical philosophy. It only demands that speculative reason end the discord with which it ensnares itself in theoretical questions, so that practical reason may have peace and security from external attacks that might make the terrain on which it desires to build contentious.

[457]

The rightful claim for freedom of the will, made even by common human reason, is founded on consciousness and admitted supposition that reason is independent of causes determined merely subjectively. Together these causes constitute what merely belongs to sensation and consequently falls under the general designation of sensibility. A person, considering himself in this way as an intelligence, places himself thereby in a different order of things and in a relation to determinate grounds of a wholly different kind. On the one hand, he thinks of himself as an intelligence endowed with a will and consequently with causality, and on the other hand, he perceives himself as a phenomenon in the world of sense (as he in fact also is), affirming that his causality is subject to external determination according to the laws of nature. Now such a person soon becomes aware that both can take place, indeed must take place, at the same time. For there is not the least contradiction in saying that a *thing in appearance* (belonging to the world of sense) is subject to certain laws of which the very same *as a thing* or a being *in itself* is independent. He must represent and think of himself in this twofold way: The first rests on the consciousness of himself as an object affected through the

21. Kant thinks there is a division of labor between theoretical and practical reason that should be respected. Theoretical reason's job is to try to make sense of the idea of freedom. That is, even if we cannot demonstrate or prove that freedom is real, theoretical reason needs to make sure that, when we assume we are free, we are not assuming something contradictory or impossible. But theoretical reason does not have the last word on free will. As Kant explains in the subsequent paragraphs, practical reason will rightly continue to presuppose that we have free will even if theoretical reason does not know what to conclude.

senses; the second, on the consciousness of himself as an intelligence, i.e., independent of sensible impressions in the use of his reason (in other words, belonging to the world of understanding).

It thus comes to pass that human beings claim the possession of a will that takes no account of anything belonging merely to desires and inclinations. On the contrary, they conceive as possible, even necessary, actions that can be performed only by disregarding all desires and sensible inclinations. The causality of such actions lies in a person as an intelligence and in the laws of effects and actions, which depend on the principles of an intelligible world. He knows nothing more of these than that pure reason alone therein, independent of sensibility, gives the law. Moreover, only in that world, where as an intelligence he is his proper self (since as a human being he is only the appearance of himself), do those laws apply to him directly and categorically. The incitements of inclinations and appetites (the whole nature of the world of sense) cannot impair the laws of his volition as an intelligence. He does not hold

[458] himself responsible for such inclinations and impulses or ascribe them to his proper self, i.e., his will. He only attributes to his will any indulgence to which he might yield if he allowed such inclinations and impulses to influence his maxims to the disadvantage of the rational laws of the will.[22]

Since practical reason *thinks* itself into a world of understanding, it does not thereby transcend its own limits as it would if it tried to enter by *intuiting* or *sensing* it. Intuition's attempt is only a negative thought with respect to the world of sense, which does not give any laws to reason in determining the will. It is positive only to the extent that this freedom as a negative determination is at the same time conjoined with a (positive) faculty and even with a causality of reason that we designate a will, namely, a faculty of acting so that the principle of the actions conforms to the essential constitution of a rational cause, i.e., the condition that the maxim should have universal validity as law. Were it to borrow an *object of*

22. Kant thinks that acting from duty shows that we can act contrary to our sensible inclinations. This is further support for his argument that we can think of ourselves as embodied beings as well as free intellects. We do not, therefore, hold ourselves responsible for merely having certain desires or motives; instead, we hold ourselves responsible for allowing them to determine our wills.

will, a motivation from the world of understanding, then it would overstep its bounds and presume to be acquainted with something of which it knows nothing. The concept of a world of the understanding is thus only a *point of view* that reason finds itself compelled to take outside the appearances, in order to *think of itself as practical*. That would not be possible if the influences of sensibility had a determining power over human beings, but it is necessary, unless he is to be denied the consciousness of himself as an intelligence and, hence, as a rational cause, active through reason, i.e., acting freely. This thought certainly involves the idea of an order and a system of laws different from that of the mechanism of nature, which belongs to the sensible world. And it makes necessary the concept of an intelligible world (i.e., the whole system of rational beings as things in themselves). But this is without the least presumption to think of it as beyond its *formal* condition only, that is, the universality of the maxims of the will as laws, and thus the will's autonomy, which alone is consistent with its freedom. On the contrary, all laws that refer to a definite object yield heteronomy, which belongs only to laws of nature and can apply only to the sensible world.[23]

[459]   Reason would overstep all its bounds if it sought to *explain how* pure reason can be practical, which would be exactly the same task as to explain *how freedom is possible*.

For we can explain nothing but that which we can reduce to laws, the object of which can be given in some possible experience. Freedom is a mere idea whose objective reality can in no way be revealed according to laws of nature and consequently not in any possible experience. For this reason, it can never be comprehended or understood, because no example can support the analogy. It holds good only as a necessary presupposition of reason in a being that believes itself conscious of a will, i.e., a faculty distinct from mere desire (a faculty of determining itself to action as an intelligence, hence by laws of reason independent of natural instincts).

23. Even though we think of ourselves as free intellects or noumenal selves, Kant is clear that we can have no insight into the nature of the noumenal self. The most we can say is that it is a point of view we find ourselves compelled to adopt.

Where determination according to the laws of nature ceases, all *explanation* ceases also. Nothing remains but *defensive* postures, rejecting the objections of those who pretend to have seen deeper into the nature of things and therefore boldly declare that freedom is impossible. We can only point out to them that their discovery of a supposed contradiction arises just from this, that in order to be able to apply the law of nature to human actions, they must necessarily consider a human being as an appearance. When we demand of them that they should also think of him as an intelligence, as a thing in itself, they still persist in considering him also as an appearance. In this view, it would no doubt be a contradiction to suppose the causality of the same subject (i.e., his will) to be separated from all the natural laws of the sensible world.

But this contradiction disappears if they would only keep in mind and admit, as is reasonable, that behind the appearances there must also lie at their root (although hidden) things in themselves, and that we cannot expect the laws of these to be the same as those that govern the appearances.

The subjective impossibility of explaining the freedom of the will is the same as the impossibility of discovering and explaining an interest* a [460] human being can take in moral laws. Nevertheless, he does actually take

---

*Interest is that by which reason becomes practical, a cause determining the will. We say of rational beings only that they take an interest in a thing, whereas irrational beings feel only sensual appetites. Reason takes a direct interest in action solely when the universal validity of its maxims on their own is sufficient to determine the will. Such an interest alone is pure. But if it can determine the will merely by means of another object of desire or the suggestion of a particular feeling of the subject, then reason takes only an indirect interest in the action, and, as reason by itself, without experience, can discover neither objects of the will nor a special feeling actuating it, this latter interest would only be empirical and not a pure rational interest. The logical interest of reason (namely, to extend its insight) is never direct but presupposes purposes for which reason is employed.

an interest in these, whose foundation within us we call the moral feeling, which some have falsely identified as the measure of our moral judgment.[24] It must rather be viewed as the *subjective* effect the law exercises on the will, whose objective principle is furnished by reason alone.

In order for a rational being to will what reason alone prescribes as an "ought" for sensibly affected rational beings, humans must undoubtedly have a faculty of reason to infuse *a feeling of pleasure* or satisfaction in the fulfillment of duty. Reason should have a causality by which it determines the sensibility according to its own principles. Discerning, i.e., making intelligible a priori, how a mere thought, which contains nothing sensible in it, can produce a sensation of pleasure or displeasure is quite impossible.[25] Like every other type of causality, we can determine nothing whatsoever a priori about this particular kind; we can only consult experience about it. Experience cannot supply us with any relation of cause and effect except between two objects of experience; so in this case, although the effect produced lies indeed within experience, the cause is still supposed to be pure reason acting through mere ideas (which offer no object to experience). It follows, then, that humans cannot possibly explain how and why the *universality of the maxim as a law*, i.e., morality, should interest us. This alone is certain: Not *because it interests* us does it have validity for us (for that would be heteronomy and dependence of practical reason on sensibility, namely, on a feeling grounding it, which could never be morally legislative). Rather, it interests us because it is valid for us as human beings, inasmuch as it had its source in our will as an intelligence, in other words, in our proper self, *and what belongs to mere appearance is necessarily subordinated by reason to the nature of the thing in itself.*

[461]

Therefore, the question "How is a categorical imperative possible?" can be answered to this extent: We can state the only presupposition on which it is possible, namely, the idea of freedom. We can also discern

24. The nature of this "moral feeling" is the topic of some debate in Kant scholarship. Kant mentions it in several places throughout his work, but what it is and how exactly it fits into his theory is unclear. Kant intends to distinguish what he means by moral feeling from what some of his predecessors meant by it.

25. Kant has been clear that the moral law is a priori and that we are not motivated to follow it by any sensible incentive. Given, however, that we are sensible creatures who act on incentives, how does the moral law cause (using Kant's term) an interest within us? As Kant argues here and in the subsequent paragraphs, we can provide no explanation because it would require knowledge that we cannot have of the noumenal self and freedom.

the necessity of this presupposition, and this is sufficient for the *practical exercise* of reason, i.e., for the conviction of the *validity of this imperative*, and hence of the moral law. No human reason can ever determine how this presupposition itself is possible. Of the presupposition, however, that the will of an intelligence is free, its *autonomy* is the essential formal condition of its determination. This is a necessary consequence. To presuppose such freedom of the will (as speculative philosophy can demonstrate) is not only entirely *possible* (not involving any contradiction to the principle of natural necessity in the connection of the appearances of the sensible world), a rational being conscious of causality through reason, i.e., of a will (distinct from desires), must *of necessity* make it practical, that is, he includes in the idea the condition of all his voluntary actions. But we must explain how pure reason can in itself be practical without the aid of any incentive of action that could be derived from any other source. The mere principle of the *universal validity of all its maxims as laws* (which would certainly be the form of a pure practical reason) can of itself supply an incentive, without any matter (object) of the will in which one could take any interest beforehand. It can produce an interest which would be called purely *moral*. In other words, *how pure reason can be practical*—to explain this is beyond the power of human reason—and all the labor and pains of seeking an explanation of that are lost.

It is just the same as if I tried to find out how freedom itself is possible as to discover the causality of will. In that case, I quit the ground of philosophical explanation, and I have no other to go on. I might indeed revel in the intelligible world, which still remains for me. Although I have a well-founded *idea* of it, I have not the least *knowledge* of it, nor can I ever attain such knowledge with all the efforts of my natural faculty of reason. It only signifies a "something" that endures when I have eliminated everything belonging to the world of sense from the actuating

[462]

principles of my will, serving merely to keep in bounds the principle of motives taken from the field of sensibility, fixing its limits and showing that it does not contain everything within itself and that there is more beyond it, but this something more I know no further. Of pure reason, which thinks this ideal, there remains, after the abstraction of all matter, i.e., knowledge of objects, nothing but the form. We must think of the practical law of the universality of maxims, and in conformity with this conception of reason in reference to a pure world of understanding, as a possible efficient cause, that is, a cause determining the will. There must be a total absence of incentives, unless this idea of an intelligible world is itself the incentive, or that in which reason primarily takes an interest, but to make this intelligible is precisely the task we cannot achieve.

Here, then, is the furthest limit of all moral inquiry. It is of great importance to determine it even on this account, in order that reason may not, being harmful to morality, on the one hand, search the world of sense for the supreme motive and an interest comprehensible but empirical. On the other hand, it may not powerlessly flap its wings unable to move in the empty space of transcendent concepts, which we call the intelligible world, and so lose itself amid pipe dreams.[26] For the rest, the idea of a pure world of understanding as a system of all intelligences, to which we ourselves belong as rational beings (although we are likewise on the other side members of the sensible world), remains always a useful and legitimate idea for the purpose of rational belief. Nonetheless, all knowledge stops at this borderline, which is useful, namely, to produce in us a lively interest in the moral law by means of the noble ideal of a universal kingdom of *ends in themselves* (rational beings).[27] We can belong to [463] this as members only when we carefully conduct ourselves according to the maxims of freedom as though they were laws of nature.

26. Kant's imagery of reason flying around in wild speculation comes from the *Critique of Pure Reason*. The conclusion to the arguments in that work is similar to the one we find here. One of the goals of this inquiry is to delineate the proper boundaries of the metaphysics of morals. As much as philosophers would like to speculate about the nature of freedom and a world of pure intellect, these are things we simply cannot know.

27. We can see the similarity between Kant's language here and the Formula of the Kingdom of Ends.

CONCLUDING REMARK

The speculative employment of reason *with respect to nature* leads to the absolute necessity of some supreme cause of *the world*. The practical employment of reason *with a view to freedom* also leads to absolute necessity, but only *of the laws of the actions* of a rational being as such. Now it is an essential *principle* of reason, however employed, to push its knowledge to a consciousness of its *necessity* (without which it would not be rational knowledge). It is, however, an equally essential *restriction* of the same reason that it can neither discern the *necessity* of what is or what happens, nor of what ought to happen, unless a condition is the ground on which it is or happens or ought to happen. In this way, however, through the restless inquiry for that condition, the satisfaction of reason is only further and further postponed. Thus, it unceasingly seeks that which is unconditionally necessary and finds itself forced to assume it, although without any means of making it comprehensible. Reason is happy enough if only it can discover a concept that supports this assumption. It is, therefore, no fault in our deduction of the supreme principle of morality, but a necessary reproach of human reason in general, that it cannot enable us to conceive the absolute necessity of an unconditional practical law (such as the categorical imperative must be). Reason cannot be blamed for refusing to explain this necessity by a condition, i.e., by means of some interest assumed as a basis. The law would then cease to be a supreme law of freedom. While we do not understand the practical unconditional necessity of the moral imperative, we nonetheless comprehend its *incomprehensibility*, and this is all that can be fairly demanded of a philosophy that strives to advance its principles to the very limit of human reason.

GLOSSARY

a posteriori: A Latin phrase meaning "dependent on experience." For Kant, the a posteriori is empirical. Although morality has an empirical dimension, it should not be derived a posteriori.

a priori: A Latin phrase meaning "independent of experience." The a priori is not mixed with anything empirical. For Kant, morality should be determined a priori.

analytic: (1) Investigating the constituent parts. (2) Knowing something based only on its definition. A statement like "bachelors are unmarried" is analytic because we know that it is true once we know that the definition of *bachelor* is "unmarried male."

apodictic: Demonstrable. The contrast would be something that we cannot prove with certainty.

critique: A critical and careful examination. Kant introduces this term primarily in *Critique of Pure Reason*.

dialectic: (1) An intellectual conflict. (2) An illusion. According to Kant, dialectics arise when we have two contrary propositions and we can furnish good reasons to accept both of them.

maxim: A subjective rule of conduct. Maxims are principles on which we act. We are supposed to subject them to the universalizability test that Kant establishes with the categorical imperative.

noumenal: How an object is in itself apart from how human beings experience it. The noumenal includes objects of perception (e.g., chairs or trees) but also selves. We have no epistemic access to the noumenal, but, according to Kant, many features of our experience and cognition make no sense without it.

phenomenal: How human beings experience an object. The phenomenal includes all the ways we represent objects to ourselves. The phenomenal description of, for example, a chair would include all its sensible qualities (e.g., it's painted green, it's three feet high, it has four legs, etc.).

practical reason: Reasoning about how to act. Kant borrows the distinction between practical and theoretical reason from Aristotle. It includes deliberation about our actions and choices, including moral ones.

propaedeutic: An introduction or the beginnings of studying a subject. Kant uses this term in several different contexts, but it does not have a more technical meaning for him.

sensibility: The mental faculty of receptivity. Sensibility includes our five senses, as well as our inclinations (desires and feelings). We have sensibility insofar as we are embodied creatures. Our sensibility is what allows us to experience the phenomenal.

synthetic: (1) Reassembling the constituent parts. (2) Knowing something by combining more than one concept. This term is a technical one for Kant. He uses it to make a distinction that he thinks many people miss. He thinks that people are prone to think that any a priori proposition is analytic. By contrast, Kant argues that there can be a priori propositions that are synthetic. Arithmetic is one of his examples. When we understand the operation $7 + 5 = 12$, it's because we combine multiple a priori concepts (like "number," "add," and "equal to") to get a new piece of information.

theoretical reason: Reasoning about what to believe. Kant takes this idea from Aristotle. Rather than deliberating and choosing how to act, theoretical reason is the domain of truth and beliefs. Theoretical reason is the subject of *Critique of Pure Reason*.

Index

About the Authors

Steven M. Cahn is professor emeritus of philosophy at the City University of New York Graduate Center. He is the author or editor of more than sixty books. Most recently, he wrote *Philosophical Adventures*; *The Road Traveled and Other Essays*; *Teaching Philosophy: A Guide*; *Inside Academia: Professors, Politics, and Policies*; and *Religion within Reason*.

Andrea Tschemplik is associate professor of philosophy at American University. Her areas of teaching and research are the history of philosophy with special emphasis on ancient and early modern philosophy. She is the author of the book *Knowledge and Self-Knowledge in Plato's "Theaetetus"* and is currently working on a monograph exploring the connection between the beautiful and the good in Plato and Kant. She also has worked on translation projects, publishing *Plato's "Republic": A Student Edition* as well as some shorter segments from Hegel's *Phenomenology*.

Krista K. Thomason is associate professor of philosophy at Swarthmore College. She received her PhD from the University of Illinois in 2009. Her areas of research include moral philosophy with an emphasis on moral emotions, Kant's moral and political theory, and social/political philosophy. Some of her work appears in *Philosophy and Phenomenological Research*, *Kantian Review*, and *European Journal of Philosophy*. She is the author of the book *Naked: The Dark Side of Shame and Moral Life*.

Mary Ann McHugh is an instructor in the Hugh Downs School of Human Communication at Arizona State University, specializing in the area of gender. She is coauthor of the 2017 edition of *Now Playing: Learning Communication through Film* and a contributing editor of *World Religions, Converging Media: A New Introduction to Mass Communication,* and *Interplay: The Process of Interpersonal Communication.*